PAPERBACK TRADER □
BOOK CREDIT

"That passionate solitude was the very soul of the genius and of the work of Michelangelo. He lived shut up in himself without any real connection with the art of his time. He despised Raphael because he said, 'All his talent came from study and not from nature.' He himself declared that he derived all his inspiration from within . . . [and] it is true that from the beginning to the end he fed on his own soul. Who knows the man, knows his work.

"The most striking thing about this extraordinarily unified nature is that it was composed of hostile worlds; a brutal materialism and serene idealism, an infatuation with pagan strength and beauty and a Christian mysticism; a mixture of physical violence and intellectual abstraction; a platonic soul in an athlete's body. That indissoluble union of opposing forces which undoubtedly caused part of his suffering was also the cause of his unique greatness. We feel that the supreme balance of his art is the result of a fierce struggle, and it is the sense of that struggle which gives to the work its heroic character. All is passion even to the abstract idea, so that idealism, which with many artists is a cause of coldness and death, is here a hearth burning with love and hate."

—FROM CHAPTER 6

ROMAIN ROLLAND

MICHELANGELO

With a New Preface by

ROBERT J. CLEMENTS

Translated by

FREDERICK STREET

COLLIER BOOKS
NEW YORK, N.Y.

This Collier Books edition is published by arrangement with Albert and Charles Boni, Inc.
Collier Books is a division of The Crowell-Collier Publishing Company

First Collier Books Edition 1962

This life of Michelangelo is published in France in the series called "Les Maîtres de l'Art." It is entirely distinct from a study of Michelangelo by Romain Rolland which appeared some time ago.

Library of Congress Catalog Card Number: 62-17571

Copyright, 1915 by Duffield & Company
Copyright © 1962 by The Crowell-Collier Publishing Company
All Rights Reserved
Hecho en los E.E.U.U.
Printed in the United States of America

Preface

WHEN ROMAIN ROLLAND, that idealist and enthusiast, admired a great personality sufficiently, he devoted a volume to him. Thus his veneration for Beethoven, Tolstóy, and Gandhi led him to compose of them sympathetic and warm biographies. His feelings for Michelangelo, moreover, were so unbounded as to incite from him two lives of the Cinquecento artist, *La Vie de Michel-Ange*, written in 1906, and *Michel-Ange* (Paris, 1905), the earlier work intended for the series "Les Maîtres de l'Art" and presented here in translation.

The later work, which has been aptly described as an "act of love," was a brief, subjective treatment which made of his idol a tragic figure no less foredoomed than a tormented figure of Greek drama. Indeed, the permeating mood was indicated by the three section-headings of the biography: "Struggle," "Abdication," and "Death." Rolland himself worried about this insistent note and finally wrote of his initial version, "At the end of this tragic history, I am troubled by a scruple. I wonder if I have perhaps, in trying to give to those who suffer a companion in distress who might sustain them, done no more than add the sorrow of this man to their own sorrows. Should I perhaps have shown, as have so many others, only the heroism of heroes, and drawn a veil over the abyss of sadness which is in them?"

Sadness and failure are certainly not lacking in the earlier version here presented, for no honest biographer could have subtracted despair and failure from an honest portrayal of Michelangelo's life. However, the account is a more balanced one, stressing more the artistic productions, and Rolland's viewpoint is that whatever ordeals this genius was obliged to endure, his tremendous contribution to art and even letters was such a fortunate one that the total picture is hardly tragic.

Romain Rolland was actually able to write a solid and factual life of Michelangelo, for the most basic researches on the artist had been completed at the time. The pioneering biographies and studies by Aurelio Gotti and Carl Justi, by the meticulous Germans Carl Frey, Hermann Grimm, and Henry Thode, had appeared, as had the two important lives by Heath Wilson and John Addington Symonds. The Germanophile Rolland admitted having drawn heavily on the two "magistral" works of Justi and Thode, despite his feeling that Thode's three volumes *Michelangelo und das Ende der Renaissance* were "Wagnerian and embarrassingly baroque."

The richest source materials of all were equally available to Rolland, the corpus of Michelangelo's poetry (now established as 302 poems and 41 fragments) and his 495 letters. The *Rime,* with their rich variety of mood and subject matter, were accessible in the near-complete edition of Carl Frey, while the letters had been edited in 1875 by Gaetano Milanesi. There were even versions in French which Rolland could have used: Lannau-Roland had translated into French by 1860 all of the extant poems (including some misreadings), and Boyer d'Agen published his *L'oeuvre littéraire de Michel-Ange* in 1911, shortly before the second version of Rolland's biography. The internationalist Romain Rolland, however, could and did read his Italian sources in the original.

Rolland's effective use of sources extended as well to Michelangelo's pronouncements and conversations on art and life recorded by his contemporaries Ascanio Condivi, Giorgio Vasari, Benvenuto Cellini, Francisco de Hollanda, Donato Giannotti, Paolo Giovio, and others, not to forget the court painter Sebastiano del Piombo, whom Michelangelo at one point wished to see "boiled in oil." Indeed, when one considers the paucity of documents on the life of Shakespeare, who was born the year of Michelangelo's death (1564), the abundance of written material concerning the master sculptor would seem to make him the more obvious subject for biography. With such rich documentation, others before Rolland wrote lives filling two or three volumes. Rolland's problem, then, was to select the most effective and symptomatic and dramatic facts—and especially quotations—to bring us close to the often enigmatic figure of Michelangelo. This selection he undertook with a large measure of success, indeed. The result is a dependable introduction to Michelangelo which has stood the test of time and will continue to do so for years to come. By adhering closely to established facts and quoting directly the spoken or written words of the master, Rolland not only achieves a commendable accuracy, but demonstrates that in the life of this particular artist, truth can be just as dramatic as fiction. He thus shuns the company of such novelists as Dmitri Merezhkowski, Sidney Alexander, and Irving Stone. And yet his accurate narrative reads as interestingly as fiction, for the force of Michelangelo's personality shines through.

When Michelangelo was buried ceremoniously in Florence's church of Santa Croce, his eulogists were unanimous in hailing him as an accomplished master of several fields. In recent times writers like Arturo Farinelli and Romain Rolland have stressed the unity of the master's several accomplishments and viewed him as outstanding not in several parallel arts, but in one transcending art which includes within itself many types of talent, just as the activities of the nine Muses were once viewed as subordinate to the one comprehensive art of "music." Michelangelo himself held a similar conviction about the overall unity of art. In the dialogues with his friends Vittoria Colonna and Francisco de Hollanda, he expressed the thought that all major and minor arts, including that of writing, were but facets of the overall art indicated by the term "design."

In the wake of Rolland and his generation, much writing has endeavored to demonstrate the unity or inseparability of the man, poet, painter, sculptor, architect, and theoretician in Michelangelo. With this unity clearly understood and accepted, we appreciate better how Michelangelo constructed a sonnet much as he executed a basic *concetto* in sculpture. We comprehend how his Platonic theory of implanted art-forms carries over into his theory on writing. We are enabled to discover more and more affinities between his artistic productions and the moods and messages of his letters and poems.

For to know the meanings of Michelangelo's works, one must know how to look for clues in each of his parallel creativities. The question once debated by the so-called New Critics concerning the need to know the life of a Homer to understand an *Iliad* has long since been decided in the case of Michelangelo. His life and his works are one. We now know, as Romain Rolland knew or intuited, that to understand to its fullest the *Last Judg-*

ment, for example, we must be familiar with the series of poems in which Michelangelo confessed his terror of dying before he had earned salvation; that to unravel the mystery of the pelt of Michelangelo with its frightening dead face ("faccia di spavento") in the grip of the Sistine Chapel's Saint Bartholomew, we must turn to the mystical renunciations of the flesh (leather, carcass, clay, dust, and the like) recurrent in his poetry. Thus the fact that Romain Rolland stays close to the historical identity of his subject, shunning the attractive primrose paths which attract the novelist-biographers, means that the reading of this biography will serve as a brief and engrossing introduction to the works, as well as the life, of Michelangelo Buonarroti.

ROBERT J. CLEMENTS

Contents

Introduction

THE LIFE OF MICHELANGELO offers one of the most striking examples of the influence that a great man can have on his time. At the moment of his birth in the second half of the fifteenth century the serenity of Ghirlandajo and of Bramante illuminated Italian art. Florentine sculpture seemed about to languish away from an excess of grace in the delicate and meticulous art of Rossellino, Disiderio, Mino da Fiesole, Agostino di Duccio, Benedetto da Maiano and Andrea Sansovino. Michelangelo burst like a thunder-storm into the heavy, overcharged sky of Florence. This storm had undoubtedly been gathering for a long time in the extraordinary intellectual and emotional tension of Italy which was to cause the Savonarolist upheaval. Nothing like Michelangelo had ever appeared before. He passed like a whirlwind, and after he had passed the brilliant and sensual Florence of Lorenzo de' Medici and Botticelli, of Verocchio and Lionardo, was ended forever. All that harmonious living and dreaming, that spirit of analysis, that aristocratic and courtly poetry, the

13

whole elegant and subtle art of the "Quattrocento," was swept away at one blow. Even after he had been gone for a long time, the world of art was still whirled along in the eddies of his wild spirit. Not the most remote corner was sheltered from the tempest; it drew in its wake all the arts together. Michelangelo captured painting, sculpture, architecture and poetry, all at once; he breathed into them the frenzy of his vigour and of his overwhelming idealism. No one understood him, yet all imitated him. Every one of his great works, the David, the cartoon for the war against Pisa, the vault of the Sistine Chapel, the Last Judgment, St. Peter's, dominated generations of artists and enslaved them. From every one of these creations radiated despotic power, a power that came above all from Michelangelo's personality and from that tremendous life which covered almost a century.

No one work can be detached from that life and studied separately. They are all fragments of one monument, and the mistake that most historians make is to mutilate this genius by dividing it into different pieces. We must try to follow the entire course of the torrent from its beginning to its end if we are to have any comprehension of its formidable unity.

Michelangelo

Chapter 1

Childhood and Youth (1475–1505)

MICHELANGELO WAS BORN on the sixth of March, 1475, at Caprese, in Casentino, of the ancient family of the Buonarroti-Simoni, who are mentioned in the Florentine chronicles from the twelfth century. His father, Lodovico di Lionardo Buonarroti-Simoni, was then Podesta of Caprese and Chiusi. His mother, Francesca di Neri di Miniato del Sera, died when he was only six years old, and some years later his father married Lucrezia Ubaldini. Michelangelo had four brothers: Lionardo, who was two years his senior; Buonarroto, born in 1477; Giovan Simoni, born in 1479; and Sigismondo, born in 1481. His foster-mother was the wife of a stone-cutter of Settignano and in later years he used to jokingly attribute his vocation to the milk upon which he had been nourished. He was sent to school in Florence under Francesco da Urbino, but he busied himself only in drawing and neglected everything else. "Because of this he greatly irritated

17

his father and his uncles, and they often beat him cruelly, for they hated the profession of an artist, and, in their ignorance of the nobility of art, it seemed a disgrace to have one in the house."[1]

The elder Buonarroti, however, was, like his son, more violent than obstinate, and he soon allowed the boy to follow his vocation. In April, 1488, Michelangelo, by the advice of Francesco Granacci, entered the studio of Domenico and David Ghirlandajo.

That was the most famous studio in Florence. Domenico was an indefatigable worker who "longed to cover with stories the entire circuit of the walls of Florence" and possessed of a calm, simple and serene spirit, satisfied merely to exist without tormenting itself over subtleties. This fortunate being, who died at forty-four, leaving an immense mass of completed work in which the magnificence and the moral force of Florence still live, was the best guide that could have been given to the young Michelangelo. Domenico was then, from 1486 to 1490, in the fulness of his power, and at work on his masterpiece, the paintings in the Tornabuoni Chapel in S. Maria Novella.

It has been said that his influence on Michelangelo amounted to nothing, and it is true that we find no direct trace of it except in two drawings in the Louvre and the Albertina. Still, exact imitation is very rare with Michelangelo. He was made of too stubborn stuff every to be much affected by masters or surroundings. He felt contempt for Raphael because he was impressionable, "and drew his superiority not from nature, but from study." I do not believe, however, that the time he spent in the school of Ghirlandajo had no effect upon him. Even if it

[1] Condivi.

did not influence his style or his method of working, he must have gained from the master of S. Maria Novella and from his wholesome work a healthy point of view and a physical and moral vigour which could have been given him by no other artist in Florence—not even the two great sculptors, Pollajuolo and Verrocchio, who were indeed not there at that time—and which acted as a powerful balance to the neuroticism of the Botticellian school. I do not doubt that Ghirlandajo helped to lay the foundations from which arose the art of the young Michelangelo devoted to the expression of force and so contemptuous of morbid sentiment.

Ghirlandajo's school was enthusiastically open-minded toward everything interesting in art. It was eclectic and encouraged intellectual curiosity. Michelangelo while he was there studied passionately both the old and the new Florentine painters and sculptors: Giotto,[2] Masaccio,[3] Donatello, Ghiberti, Benedetto da Majano, Mino da Fiesole, Antonio Rossellino and possibly, even at that time, Jacopo della Quercia and also the Flemish and the German artists, then very much in vogue in Italy, especially at the court of the Medici.[4] He made a copy in colour of Martin Schongauer's Temptation of St. Anthony and went to the Florentine fish-market to take notes for

[2] Drawings in the Louvre from the frescoes of Santa Croce.

[3] Munich. Drawings from the frescoes of the Carmine.

[4] In the collection of the Medici a St. Jerome by Van Eyck was valued at forty ducats, the Giottos and Fra Angelicos at only ten ducats. The Flemings were no less appreciated at Urbino where Justus of Ghent had painted, whose frescoes were copied by Raphael when he was a child, and at Rome where Jan Ruysch, twenty years later, was to work on the Stanze, and throughout the kingdom of Naples—not to mention the great collection of Flemish pictures in the north of Italy, like those of Cardinal Grimani at Venice, and of Cardinal Bembo at Padua.

it. Later on he contemptuously disowned Flemish realism, but a trace of it was left in him always and in many of his drawings there appears a certain taste, extraordinary in an idealist, for types of marked naturalism which are sometimes trivial or almost caricature.

Condivi asserts that these first attempts of Michelangelo met with such success that Ghirlandajo grew jealous.

"To take from him the credit of this copy (of the Schongauer) Ghirlandajo used to say that it came out of his atelier, as if he had had a part in it. This jealousy showed very clearly when Michelangelo asked him for the book of drawings wherein he had sketched shepherds with their flocks and dogs, landscapes, monuments, ruins, etc., and he refused to lend it to him. As a matter of fact, he always had the reputation of being rather jealous, because of his disagreeable treatment not only of Michelangelo, but also of his own brother, for when he saw the latter making good progress and showing great promise, he sent him to France, not so much for his benefit, as has been alleged, as that he himself might remain first in his art at Florence. I have mentioned this," adds Condivi, "because it has been said to me that Domenico's son was in the habit of attributing the divine excellence of Michelangelo to the training given by his father, who really did not help him in any way. It is true that Michelangelo never complained of him, but on the contrary praised him as much for his art as for his conduct."

It is very difficult to say how much is true in this story. I am reluctant to ascribe so contemptible a jealousy to Ghirlandajo, and repeat it only because of the last line where Condivi is constrained to remark on the esteem which Michelangelo, when he was an old man, expressed for his former master. Such admiration for other artists is too rare with him not to have especial weight in this case.

There is no doubt that a disagreement did arise between the master and the scholar, for though Michelangelo had in 1488 signed a contract of apprenticeship which stipulated that he should remain three years with Ghirlandajo,[5] the very next year he went with his friend Granacci into the school of Bertoldo.

Bertoldo, a pupil of Donatello, was director of the School of Sculpture and of the Museum of Antiquities maintained by Lorenzo de' Medici in the gardens of S. Marco. I think that the real reason why Michelangelo separated himself from Ghirlandajo was that after a year of feeling his way he had just discovered the essence of his genius and was drawn toward sculpture with irresistible force. It was really from painting that he was separating himself and never afterward did he consider it as his art. We might almost say that if painting has immortalised him it is in spite of himself. He never wished to be considered as anything but a sculptor.[6]

Two things drew him to Bertoldo: the hope of finding the tradition of Donatello and the fascination of the antique. He found something even more valuable there in the friendship of the prince and of the élite of the Florentine thinkers. Lorenzo took an interest in him, lodged him in the palace and admitted him to his son's table, and in this way Michelangelo found himself at the very heart of the Renaissance, in the midst of the humanists and the poets and in intimate relation with all whom Italy counted most noble; with Pico della Mirandola, with Pulci, Benevieni and especially with Poliziano, "who loved him

[5] Michelangelo was to receive six florins the first year, eight the second and ten the third.

[6] "On the 10th of May, 1508," as he wrote at a later time, "I Michelangelo, *sculptor,* began to work on the paintings of the Sistine Chapel."

greatly and urged him to study, although that was hardly necessary."[7]

Surrounded by this atmosphere of lofty paganism he became intoxicated with the classic idea and became himself a pagan; he made the heroic forms of Greece live again while putting into them his own savage vigour. Following the suggestions of Poliziano he wrought the bas-relief of the Combat of the Centaurs and the Lapithæ of the Casa Buonarroti, in which the figures are athletic and struggling and the faces impassive and proud. He carved the bestial face of the Laughing Satyr with its violent and strained expression as of one who was not used to laughter, and a little later the relief of Apollo and Marsyas.

Nevertheless this paganism did not touch his Christian faith at all. The struggle that was to endure almost all his life had already begun within him between those two hostile worlds which he vainly tried to reconcile. In 1489 and 1490 Savonarola began in Florence his fiery sermons on the Apocalypse and Michelangelo went to hear them with all the rest of Lorenzo's circle. He had been brought up very religiously by his father, a kind, God-fearing man of the old style, and his brother Lionardo in 1491, under the influence of Savonarola, entered the Monastery of the Dominicans at Pisa.

He could not remain indifferent to the burning words of a prophet who was like an elder brother of the prophets of the Sistine and whose sombre visions and fiery purity must have pierced the heart of the youth who listened to the preaching in S. Marco or the Duomo. I am convinced, nevertheless, that historians have very much

[7] He had for his companions at Bertoldo's, Granacci, the sculptors Rustici, Baccio di Monte Lupo and Andrea del Monte-Sansovino, the painters Niccolo Soggi, Lorenzo di Credi, Giuliano Bugiardini and the brutal Torrigiano dei Torrigiani, whose blow left its mark on Michelangelo's face for life.

exaggerated the effect of this influence on Michelangelo. In the beginning he certainly did not feel very strongly the heroic grandeur of the frail little preacher who from his high pulpit launched his lightnings against pope and princes. His first impression seems to have been almost entirely one of terror; he did not escape from the contagion of fear which seized the entire city at the thunder of the gloomy prophecies which held the bloody sword of God suspended over Italy and which filled the streets of Florence with people weeping madly. When at last there came the new Cyrus, foretold by the monk of S. Marco, Charles VIII, King of France, Michelangelo was seized with panic and fled to Venice (1494).

These superstitious terrors, irrational and uncontrollable, which reappeared more than once in Michelangelo's life do not prove anything in favour of his Savonarolaism. It might be supposed on the contrary that a true disciple of Savonarola would have remained beside his master rather than have abandoned him in the hour of danger. These panics which he could not control prove nothing but the unhealthy over-excitement of his nerves, which his reason fought against in vain all his life. It would be hard to find in his work at that period any appreciable effect of the ideas of Savonarola. The impassive Virgin with the robust child—the bas-relief in bronze of the Casa Buonarroti—is far more a school piece by a pupil of Donatello than a religious work. What we know of the little wooden crucifix, carved in 1494 for the prior of the Convent of S. Spirito, shows us the artist without mysticism and with a passion for the observation of nature, who was eagerly studying anatomy from corpses until their putrefaction made him ill and forced him to stop. At Bologna, where he lived in 1449 after his flight from Florence, and where he heard of the results of Savonarola's preachings—the expulsion of the Medici, the death of Pico della Mirandola and of Poliziano and the scattering of the little circle of Florentine poets and philosophers—he spent his time in reading Petrarch, Boccaccio and Dante to his protector, the noble Gianfrancesco Aldovrandi, and when he worked at the Arca (tabernacle) of S. Domenico it was to carve that athletic angel, superb and expressionless, which contrasts so strikingly with the pious figure of Niccolo dell' Arca to which it is the pendant. He was evidently much more occupied in studying and assimilating the imposing manner of Jacopo della Quercia, his indolent and heavy but powerful Siennese precursor, than in meditating on the prophecies of Savonarola.

He returned to Florence in 1495, and arrived in the midst of the struggle of the two parties, the "Arrabtiati" and the "Piagnoni," at the very height of the carnival. He was consulted about the construction of the hall of the Grand Council in the Palace of the Signory. The Virgin of Manchester which suggests the school of Ghirlandajo may be attributed to this period, and also the Entombment of the National Gallery, which with all its sad grandeur is proud and cold.

Michelangelo left Florence in June, 1496. He went to Rome and in that town so full of classic memories he absorbed himself in classic works. It is fair to say that he was never so pagan as from 1492 to 1497, the years during which the tragedy of Savonarola was enacted. This is the period of the colossal Hercules[8] in marble (1492), of the famous sleeping Cupid, wrought in the very heart of mystical Florence—and sold as an antique to Cardinal Riaro (1496)—of the large Cupid of the South Kensing-

[8] At first in the Strozzi Palace, then bought in 1529 by Francis I and placed at Fontainebleau, it disappeared in the seventeenth century.

ton, of the Dying Adonis of the Museo Nazionale and of the Drunken Bacchus which E. Guillaume calls the nearest to the antique of all modern works. These last statues, made in Rome the very year of the *Bruciamento delle Vanità*, when the Florentine "Piagnoni" danced in fanatic zeal around bonfires of works of art, seem almost like a defiance launched against the puritanism of Savonarola. His older brother, Lionardo, a monk at Viterbo, who was forced to flee from his monastery because of his Savonarolaist convictions, joined him in Rome and Michelangelo gave him some money with which to return to Florence, but he did not go with him. The ever-growing danger which threatened the prophet and his followers did not draw him back to his country and Savonarola's death—he was burnt in May, 1498—has not left a trace in any of his letters.[9]

I do not mean to say that he was entirely untouched by that grand and tragic drama. He was by nature silent and never spoke of what he felt most deeply, and he was also prudent and afraid of compromising himself. If Savonarola's ideas did have some influence on him it was at a later time when, in his advanced age, under the influence of strong and deep friendships, the disillusions of life and the fear of the hereafter, religious preoccupations gained with him the place of first importance. He was not among those who, like Botticelli, in 1498, consented to the dethronement of the pagan pride of the Renaissance. Religious he certainly was and a Christian as always, but his proud Christianity was not that of the rest of the world.

[9] I find it impossible to recognise, as Thode does, an allusion to the death of Savonarola in a letter of 1508, when Michelangelo, hearing that his father had been slandered by his brother, writes, "I have not received worse news in ten years." Nothing justifies us in believing that Michelangelo is not merely alluding to other family difficulties.

He was never understood by his own time. Even when he was painting the Last Judgment, and his faith was most ardent, he must have scandalised the devout. He was altogether a Platonist. He could have said with Lorenzo de' Medici and his illustrious friends of the gardens of S. Marco that "without studying Plato one could neither be a good citizen nor an enlightened Christian." Savonarola undoubtedly admired and loved Plato. Still he felt the object of art to be religious edification and showed that ideal to artists in "the face of a pious woman when she is praying, illuminated by a ray of divine beauty."[10] Michelangelo despised that art made for the devout and left it to the Flemings.[11] He had a horror of sentimentality and almost of sentiment. "True painting," he said, "never will make any one shed a tear."[12]

It should contain no expression of religion or worship, for "good painting is religious and devout in itself. Among the wise nothing more elevates the soul or better raises it to adoration than the difficulty of attaining the perfection which approaches God and unites itself to Him."[13] He believed himself to be more religious in creating beautiful, harmonious human bodies than in searching for a psychological or moral expression intended "for women, especially for the old or the very young, or for monks, nuns and those who are deaf to true harmony."[14] The Pietà of St. Peter's, undertaken the year of Savonarola's death, has a more Christian character than the

[10] Sermons on Amos and Zachariah.

[11] See the "Dialogues de la Peinture" of Francis of Holland, who relates the conversations between Michelangelo and Vittoria Colonna in Rome in 1538-39.

[12] Beethoven wrote in the same way to Bettina Brentano in 1810: "most men are moved by beauty, but that is not the nature of artists. Artists are fashioned of fire—they do not weep."

[13] Francis of Holland *ibid.*

[14] *Ibid.* The passage applies to Flemish painting in general.

earlier works of Michelangelo, but this Christianity is still far from conforming to the expressive and pathetic ideal of the artists of the fifteenth century, or from the tragic expression and agony of suffering of the virgins of Donatello, Signorelli or Mantegna. Very different indeed is the noble harmony of this group and the calm beauty of the young Virgin on whose knees rests the supple body of Christ relaxed like that of a sleeping child. Even though Michelangelo explained the eternal youth of the Virgin[15] by an idea of chivalric mysticism it is evident that at that time the desire for beauty was as strong in his heart as any regard for faith and that there was a certain relationship between these beautiful Gods of Calvary and those of Olympus whose charm had intoxicated him.

Michelangelo spent two years on the Pietà.[16] In the spring of 1501 he returned to Florence and there met

[15] "Do you know," said Michelangelo to Condivi, "that chaste women remain much more fresh than those who are not chaste. How much more, therefore, must this be true of the Virgin who never entertained the least immodest thought which might have troubled her body. I would put this even more strongly. I believe that this freshness and flower of youth which she received in a natural manner was preserved for her in a supernatural one, so that the virginity and the eternal purity of the Mother of God could be demonstrated to the world. Such a miracle was not necessary for the Son. Quite the contrary, for if it had to be shown that the Son of God was made incarnate in man and that he had suffered all that men suffer except sin, it was not necessary to make the human disappear behind the divine, but it was better rather to let the human follow its nature in such a way that he should appear to have the age that he really had. Do not be surprised, therefore, if for these reasons I have represented the Very Holy Virgin, the Mother of God, much younger than her years would require and if I have given the Son his real age."

[16] Contract of August 26, 1498, with the French Cardinal, Jean de Groslaye de Villiers, Abbot of S. Denis, Ambassador of Charles VIII, who had ordered it for the chapel of the kings of France (Chapel of S. Petronille) at St. Peter's.

Cardinal Piccolomini, with whom he signed a contract to deliver in three years' time, for the sum of five hundred ducats, fifteen figures of apostles and saints for the Piccolomini altar in the Cathedral of Sienna. This was the first of those overpowering commissions which Michelangelo never hesitated to undertake in the first intoxication of his imagination without any just estimate of his powers and which weighed on him all his life, like remorse. In 1504 he had delivered only four of the figures and sixty years later in 1561 he was still tormented by the thought of this unfulfilled contract.

Another undertaking, more tempting to him by its very difficulty, took entire possession of him a few months after he had made the agreement with Cardinal Piccolomini.

A gigantic block of marble had been delivered in 1464 to Agostino di Duccio by the Board of Works of S. Maria del Fiore to be used for the statue of a prophet. The work had been interrupted at this point. The Gonfalonier Soderini wanted to entrust the completion of it to Lionardo da Vinci, but in August, 1502, it was given to Michelangelo and he set to work on it at once. From that block of marble came forth the colossal David. By January 25, 1504, the work was completed and a commission of artists among whom were Botticelli, Filippino Lippi, Lionardo da Vinci and Perugino was considering where it should be placed. They hesitated between the Loggia dei Lanzi and the entrance of the Palace of the Signory. The latter position was decided upon at the expressed preference of Michelangelo. The architects of the Duomo, Simone del Pollojuolo (Cronaca), Antonio da San Gallo, Baccio d'Agnolo and Bernardo della Cecca were charged with the transportation of the enormous mass of stone which was placed in position on the eighth of June, 1504, on the left of the entrance to the Palazzo Vecchio where until then the Judith of Donatello had stood.

To-day the David is in the Accademia delle Belle Arti in Florence. There it is in too confined a space. That colossus needs the open air, he stifles under the roof of a Palace and his disproportion to everything around him is shocking. We can perhaps judge better what he really is from the reproduction in bronze, which on the hill of San Miniato raises its inspiring silhouette above the town. There the irregularity of the details disappears in the impression of the whole. Incredible energy emanates from that gigantic force in repose—from that great face in the small head, and from that huge body with the slender waist, thin arms and the enormous hands with swollen veins and heavy fingers.

All of Michelangelo is there in that mixture of proud nobility and almost barbarous vulgarity. He is all there, and he only, entirely regardless of his subject. The head of the David with its wrinkled forehead, thick eyebrows and scornful lips—a type that he often used afterward—is, like the heads of Lorenzo and of Giuliano de' Medici, a lyric work into which Michelangelo poured his own sadness, disdain and melancholy.

Michelangelo had not waited to finish this work before accepting other commissions which he was to abandon along the way. In 1502 a David[17] in bronze for Pierre de Rohan, Maréchal de Gié, the favorite of Louis XII, which in the end was finished by Benedetto da Rovezzano in 1507 and sent, after the disgrace of Rohan, to

---

[17] This David was placed in the centre of the court of the Château de Bury and moved in the sixteenth century to the Château de Villeroy near Mennecy from where it afterward disappeared. The figure was life-size, with the head of Goliath at its feet; a pen-and-ink sketch in the Louvre is all that is left of it.

the new royal favourite, Florimond Robertet, Secretary of Finance.

In 1503 he undertook twelve statues for the Cathedral of Florence, but began only one, a St. Matthew, which was never finished and is now in the Accademia delle Belle Arti. His vacillating, uncertain genius, wherein discouragement succeeded to enthusiasm, drove him into planning works with fierce energy and then almost immediately so diverted his attention that he could not force himself to finish them.

In 1504 the Florentine Signory brought him into competition with another great irresolute, Lionardo da Vinci, whose universal intellectual curiosity was, no less than the temperament of Michelangelo, an eternal obstacle to the achievement of his great undertakings. The two men seem to have met about 1495. They could not have understood each other very well, for they both stood alone, each in his own way. Lionardo was now fifty-two years old. When he was thirty he had left Florence, where the bitterness of the political and religious passions was unbearable to his delicate and slightly timid nature and to his serene and sceptical intelligence which was interested in everything but refused to take sides. Driven back to Florence by the death or ruin of his protectors, the Duke of Milan and Cæsar Borgia, he came into contact there from the very first with Michelangelo entirely absorbed in his own faith and passions, however changing they might be, and who, while he hated the enemies of his party and of his faith, hated still more those who had neither party nor faith. Brutally and publicly, on many occasions, Michelangelo made Lionardo feel his aversion for him.

When the Gonfalonier Soderini put the two in direct competition in a common work, the decoration of the Council Hall in the Palace of the Signory, the rivalry was intense. In May, 1504, Lionardo began the cartoon of the

Battle of Anghiari. In August, 1504, Michelangelo received the order for the cartoon for the Battle of Cascine. Florence was divided into two camps keenly enthusiastic for one or the other of the rivals. Time has made them equal, for both pictures have disappeared. Michelangelo's cartoon, finished in March, 1505, was apparently destroyed about 1512, during the disturbances in Florence which resulted from the return of the Medici, and even the fragments which in 1575 were still preserved by the Strozzi in Mantua have been lost.[18]

As for Lionardo's fresco, he succeeded in destroying it himself. He took it into his head to try to perfect the technique of fresco and he gave himself up once more to his evil spirit of invention and once more everything was lost. He tried a glaze of oil which did not hold, and the painting which he abandoned in 1506 in discouragement by 1550 no longer existed.

The two cartoons of Lionardo and Michelangelo had time, nevertheless, to exert a blinding fascination over all Italian painting. They formed the style and influenced the thought of artists from 1506 on but without being able to

[18] Carducho saw some fragments in 1633 in the possession of the Viceroy of Naples. Marc-Antonio engraved in 1510 the celebrated episode of the bathers, using for a background a landscape of Lucas van Leyden. Agostino Veneziano made another engraving of it in 1523–24. Aristotele da San Gallo made a drawing of the whole composition and in 1542 made from the drawing an oil-painting (Holkham Castle, England). There exist many fragmentary studies of the work in the Albertina Collection at Vienna, the Accademia at Venice, the Louvre and Oxford University. They can be put together by following a drawing of Daniele da Volterra in the Uffizi. The battle included, besides the episode of the bathers, a cavalry combat. "Si vedono infiniti combattendo di cavallo cominciare la zuffa," says Vasari. The moment chosen was the one when a trumpet call gave the alarm to the Florentines, surprised while bathing by the Pisans.

transmit their own grandeur. Lionardo, who had a cavalry combat to represent, reasoned out coldly, as nearly as we can tell,[19] all the circumstances of a battle and then reproduced them with his marvellous lucidity which was perhaps a little too analytic to interpret the excitement of passion.

Michelangelo, who was given an episode of the war of 1364 against the Pisans under the leadership of the condottiere John Hawkwood (Giovanni Acuto) had intentionally turned his back on history and the real subject and painted naked men bathing, noble in form and free in movement, in the classic manner.[20]

The two masterpieces contained each of them the germ of a different danger; in Lionardo's the excess of analysis, in Michelangelo's the excess of abstraction. This last was the most dangerous of the two but both were of the intellect and agreed in substituting for the charm of life and of real and spontaneous movement the formula of types and of logical action.

The influence of this work became at once universal and tyrannical. Benvenuto Cellini says in 1559: "The cartoon of Michelangelo was placed in the palace of the Medici, that of Lionardo in the Hall of the Pope. As long as they remained there they were the school of the world." Raphael copied them many times from October, 1504,

[19] Especially from the notes where Lionardo described a battle in his "Thatteto della Pittura," II, 145, a combination of photographic exactness and academic rationalism.

[20] Never had so many nudes been seen in one composition except in the Last Judgment at Orvieto. Michelangelo pushed so far his contempt not only for any psychological analysis, but for all dramatic probability, that he introduced into the midst of the composition a naked man lying down and turning over lazily without seeming to take any notice of the tumult around him. It was a classic bas-relief radiant with heroic beauty and regardless alike of subject and feeling.

until July, 1505. Fra Bartolommeo was inspired by them and Andrea del Sarto, when he was very young, spent whole days in studying them. Among the artists who taught themselves in that school are Perino del Vaga, Rosso, Battista Franco, Salviati, Vasari, Bronzino, Ridolfo Ghirlandajo, Cellini, Pontormo, Jacopo Sansovino, Franciabigio, Aristotele da San Gallo, F. Granacci, Bandinelli, Morto da Feltro, Lorenzetto—almost all the famous men of the period. This influence was certainly more dangerous than useful. The first fruits of it were the sudden unpopularity—almost like a decree of exile of all the charming primitive painters, like Pinturicchio[21] and Signorelli[22] at Rome (1508) just after their masterpieces at Sienna and Orvieto and Perugino at Florence (1504) four years after the exquisite decoration of the *Cambio* of Perugia—and the loss of so much grace, elegance and vigour sacrificed to a form of beauty undoubtedly superior, but to which every one can not attain. Instead of giving them a broader point of view, the admiration for Lionardo and Michelangelo narrowed and limited their followers. During 1508–1509 Pope Julius II had the frescoes of Sodoma, Perugino, Signorelli and Piero della Francesca put aside to leave space for Raphael. Thenceforth everyone was governed by the same ideal, and whoever felt in himself fancy, imagination and youth gave them up in favour of an attempt at breadth and power which were not for him. Filippino Lippi renounced his serious simplicity for pedantic dilettanteism and affected

[21] Frescoes of Pinturicchio in the library of the Cathedral at Sienna, finished in 1507.

[22] Frescoes of Signorelli in the chapel of the Cathedral of Orvieto, finished in December, 1504. It is well known with what brutality Michelangelo showed on many occasions his contempt for Signorelli and for Perugino.

gestures. Instead of being the first in the second rank
Lorenzo di Credi, Ridolfo Ghirlandajo, Rafaellino del
Garbo and Piero di Cosimo preferred to be the last of
the first rank.

The same rivalry which had brought about the competition between Michelangelo and Lionardo in the Council Hall appears again in a series of works which belong
to this Florentine period (1501–1505). These are repre-
sentations of the "Holy Family" in which Michelangelo
attempts to solve the same problem of composition as
Lionardo and Fra Bartolommeo in placing the figures in
a circle. Such are the two circular bas-reliefs, the Madonna and Child of the Museo Nazionale made for Taddeo Taddei and the Holy Family of the Academy of Fine
Arts in London made for Bartolommeo Pitti. Chief of
them all is the great picture in distemper of the Holy
Family of the Uffizi painted for Agnolo Doni—a heroic
work filled with the lofty serene life of Olympus and the
Parthenon. The painting is the most carefully executed
of all Michelangelo's. The colouring, blue, rose, orange
and golden brown, has an effect that is rather inharmo-
nious, but young and fresh. The aerial perspective is
mediocre and the composition shows as usual Michelangelo's supreme contempt for the sentiment of the subject. He has filled the background with graceful nude
figures simply because he considered them to be beautiful
—"per mostrare maggiormente l'arte sua essere grandis-
sima," says Vasari, and except for the type of face used
for St. Joseph there is nothing religious about the group
of the Holy Family. The impression is religious, nevertheless, through its grace, sweetness and proud strength. We
feel that Michelangelo desired to contrast the puritan and
virile sobriety of this work with the voluptuous languor of
the art of Lionardo.

The calm Madonna of Bruges belongs also to this period. This was bought in 1506 by two Flemish merchants, John and Alexander Mouscron, who placed it in their chapel where Dürer had already seen it during his travels in Belgium in 1521.

Chapter 2

Michelangelo and Julius II (1505–1513)

IN MARCH, 1505, Michelangelo was called to Rome by Pope Julius II. Then began the heroic period of his life and the "tragedy" of the monument of Julius II which was not to end until forty years later. The pope and the artist, both of them proud and violent, were well fitted to work together—so long as their ideas did not conflict. Their brains seethed with tremendous ideas. The first years of their friendship were a feverish delirium of plans. Julius II was on fire with enthusiasm for the plan for his tomb which Michelangelo submitted to him. It was to be a mountain of architecture with more than forty statues, some of them of colossal size, and with many bronze reliefs. "Michelangelo's design pleased the pope so much," says Condivi, "that he sent him at once to Carrara (April, 1505) with an order to cut as much marble as he needed. . . . Michelangelo stayed more than eight months in the mountains with two servants and a horse."

He was the victim of superhuman exaltation and in his enthusiasm dreamt of carving a whole mountain. In December, 1505, he returned to Rome, where the blocks of marble which he had chosen had already begun to arrive from Carrara. They were unloaded at La Ripa and then transported to the Piazza di San Pietro behind S. Caterina, where Michelangelo lived. "The mass of the stones was so great that they aroused the wonder and joy of the pope." Michelangelo set to work. "The pope in his impatience came constantly to see him and conferred with him over the monument and other works, with as much familiarity as if he had been his brother. In order that he might visit him the more easily he had a drawbridge thrown across from the gallery of the Vatican to Michelangelo's house which gave him a secret passage."

But this favour did not last. The character of Julius II was as passionate and as changeable as that of Michelangelo. His mind, always in a ferment, took up in rapid succession and ever with the same eagerness the most varied projects. Another idea drove the plan for the tomb from his mind. In order that he might gain immortal glory by one gigantic work he decided to reconstruct St. Peter's. He was encouraged in this by enemies of Michelangelo, who himself writes in 1542:[1]

"All the difficulties which arose between the pope and myself were the work of Bramante and of Raphael. It was their jealousy that kept him from having his tomb made while he was still alive. They tried to ruin me. Raphael had good reason for doing this, since all that he knew of art he learnt from me."

It is not easy to say how far Raphael was carried along

---

[1] At the end of a memorial in which he went over the whole history of the monument of Julius II in order to clear himself from blame. (Lettere di M. A.B., Ed. G. Milanesi, Florence, 1875, cdxxxv, p. 494.)

by the party of Bramante, who was his friend and fellow-countryman, but there is no doubt that Bramante was chiefly responsible for the check to Michelangelo's great undertaking and that he profited by his absence in Carrara to destroy his influence over the pope.

"The marks of his favour which Julius II had showered on Michelangelo," says Condivi, "resulted, as often happens at courts, in exciting jealousy against him, and, following the jealousy, endless persecution. Bramante, the architect, who was dear to the pope, made him change his plans. He reminded him of the popular superstition that it was of bad augury to build your tomb while you were still alive, and other stories of the same kind. Bramante was driven to do this, not only through jealousy, but from fear that Michelangelo's knowledge would reveal his own mistakes. For Bramante, as everyone knows, was much given to pleasure and very dissipated. The salary he received from the pope, though it was great, was not nearly enough for him, so that he tried to make more out of his work by constructing walls of bad material and neither solid nor strong enough for their height and thrust. Anyone can prove this by the construction of St. Peter's, or the Belvedere gallery, or the cloister of S. Pietro in Vinculi and other buildings which he erected and which it has been necessary to support all over again and to strengthen with buttresses,[2] either because they have fallen down or because they very soon would have done so. Bramante realised that Michelangelo would have discovered his mistakes, and so he always tried to keep him away from Rome and to deprive him of the pope's favour and of the influence which he had gained over the pope by his works. For it is clear that if

[2] Thode confirms this opinion, which was also held by Serlio in the sixteenth century, in regard to the construction of St. Peter's.

the tomb of Julius II had been actually undertaken Michelangelo would have stood out supreme over all other artists, however famous they might be, for he would then have had a vast field in which to show what he could do."

Bramante succeeded. In January, 1506, Julius II ordered the reconstruction of St. Peter's. The tomb was abandoned and Michelangelo was not only humiliated and disappointed, but in debt, according to what he says himself:

"When the pope changed his mind and the boats arrived with the marble from Carrara I had to pay the charge of transport myself. And as at this same time the stone-cutters who had come from Florence for the tomb also arrived at Rome and I had had the house which Julius had given me behind S. Caterina prepared for them, I found myself without money and greatly embarrassed. I urged the pope as strongly as I could to continue the construction of the tomb and then one morning when I wished to talk with him about it he had me put out by a groom."

Then it was that the famous flight to Florence took place. Michelangelo, outraged by this affront, took horse and fled from Rome and refused to return in spite of the messengers which the pope sent after him. The indignity of the affront was not, by his own account, the only reason for his flight. In a letter to Giuliano da San Gallo he implies that his life was in danger from Bramante's threats.

"That was not the only reason for my leaving. There was still another which I would rather not speak about. It is enough to say that it made me think that if I stayed in Rome that town would more likely be my tomb than that of the pope. And that was the reason for my sudden departure."

Nothing justifies us in believing that Bramante had

thought of having recourse to a crime, but it was enough that Michelangelo believed him to be capable of it and, in one of those accesses of sudden terror which contrast so strangely with the stubborn boldness of his genius, he ran away. Moreover, Bramante understood perfectly how to terrorise his rivals and to make life near him impossible for them. Only a little while after Michelangelo Giuliano da San Gallo, who was Bramante's last rival at St. Peter's, also had to flee.

There was, however, still another reason for the sudden departure of Michelangelo, and though he himself has taken good care to say nothing about it, I am surprised that the historians have not brought it out more clearly. Michelangelo fled on the seventeenth of April, 1506. On the eighteenth of April there took place the solemn ceremony of the laying of the first stone of St. Peter's. This is the true reason for his sudden withdrawal; he did not want to be present at the triumph of his enemy.

He had hardly left before Bramante so arranged matters that he could not come back. He ruined his work and his fortunes.

"That affair," writes Michelangelo, "caused me a loss of more than a thousand ducats. When I left Rome there arose a great riot because of the shame put upon the pope, and almost all the blocks of marble which I had on the square of St. Peter's were taken from me, especially the smaller pieces, which made it necessary for me later on to begin the whole work over again."

Nevertheless Julius II was furious at the revolt of his sculptor and sent letter after letter to the Signory of Florence where Michelangelo had betaken himself. The Signory, anxious not to compromise themselves, tried to persuade Michelangelo to take once more the road to Rome, but he would do nothing of the kind. He had tranquilly taken up his work on the cartoon of The Battle, the

Twelve Apostles for the cathedral and the Madonna of Bruges, and he stubbornly persisted in his unwillingness to return. He proposed his own terms and pretended to be working on the tomb of Julius II at Florence. When, toward the end of August, 1506, Julius II went to war with Perugia and Bologna and grew more importunate in his demands Michelangelo had the idea of expatriating himself. He thought of going to Turkey, where the Sultan, through the Franciscans, invited him to come to Constantinople and build a bridge at Pera.[3]

In the end he had to give in, and in the latter part of November, 1506, he went, much against his will, to Bologna, where Julius II had just entered the town as a conqueror. There took place that famous interview when the pope, angry and scolding, divided between the desire of punishing the rebel and the fear of losing the artist whom he valued, poured out his wrath on an unlucky bishop who was present, and forgave Michelangelo.

Unfortunately, Michelangelo in order to make his peace with the pope, had to submit to his caprices and to that all-powerful will which had now turned in a new direction. It was no longer a question of the tomb, but of a colossal bronze statue which Julius wished to have raised to himself in Bologna.

In vain Michelangelo protested that he understood nothing about the casting of bronze. He had two assistants, Lopo and Lodovico, come from Florence, and a foundryman, Bernadino d'Antonio dal Ponte. But he could never get along with any assistant. He fell out with Lodovico and Lopo, who stole from him; then the found-

---

[3] In 1519 we find traces of new correspondence between Michelangelo and Turkey. A certain Tommaso di Tolfo of Adrianople begs him to come to Turkey and to paint some pictures for the "Seigneur of Adrianople, who is a connoisseur in art and has bought an antique."

ryman turned out to be incapable and in June, 1507, the casting failed.

"The figure came out only as far down as the waist. Everything had to be done over again."

Fifteen months were spent in the midst of all kinds of troubles and mortifications. Michelangelo was busy with his work until February, 1508. He nearly ruined his health over it, and he wrote to his brother that he would never be in condition to make such an effort again during his life. For so great a struggle, the result was miserable. The statue of Julius II, raised on February 21, 1508, in front of the facade of S. Petronio remained there only four years.[4] In December, 1511, it was destroyed on the return of the Bentivogli, and Alphonso d'Este had his bombardier Quirino cast a cannon from its fragments.

Michelangelo returned to Rome and Julius II laid upon him another task not less unexpected and not less hazardous. He ordered the sculptor, who never painted except with reluctance and who knew nothing of the technique of fresco, to paint the ceiling of the Sistine Chapel. He had already talked with him about it before the rupture in 1506 and the disinclination of Michelangelo for this work had something to do with his flight to Florence. This may be inferred from the letter of a friend of Michelangelo written in May, 1506, which shows that Bramante, satisfied by the withdrawal of his rival, justified him for refusing the burden of this heavy undertaking.

"Last Saturday evening," writes Pietro Rosselli, "when the pope was supping, he called Bramante and said, 'San Gallo is going tomorrow to Florence and he will bring back Michelangelo.' Bramante answered, 'Holy Father, Michelangelo will do nothing of the kind. I have talked a

---

[4] The statue was seven brasses (11.34 metres) high and the Pope was represented as seated.

great deal with him and he has often said to me that he would not undertake the chapel which you wished to entrust to him. He asks to be allowed with your permission to devote himself entirely to scupture, for he wants to have nothing to do with painting.' He added, 'Holy Father, I do not think he has the courage to undertake the work, for he has had little experience in the painting of figures, and these must be painted on the ceiling and foreshortened, which is very different from painting on the ground.' The pope answered, 'If he does not come he will be treating me badly, and for that reason I think he will return.' I threw myself into the conversation and there in the pope's presence replied properly to that fellow and spoke for you as you would surely have spoken for me. Bramante remained silent, realising that he had made a mistake in saying what he had. I went on in these words: 'Holy Father, that man has never exchanged a word with Michelangelo, and if what he says is true you can cut my head off. He has never talked with him, and I am sure that Michelangelo will come back if Your Holiness wishes it.'" When Michelangelo returned Bramante changed his tactics. As Michelangelo's friends had imprudently asserted that he could accomplish this task for which, as Bramante knew better than any one else, he was entirely unprepared, Bramante pretended to believe this and forced his rival into a position where he had to accept the commission. A failure would have been particularly serious to Michelangelo just then since in that same year, 1508, Raphael began his incomparable painting of the Stanze and Michelangelo had either to surpass him or be entirely eclipsed. This at least is what Condivi asserts.

"Bramante and his other rivals suggested to the pope to make Michelangelo paint the ceiling of the chapel of Pope Sixtus IV by persuading him that he would do marvels there. They did him this service maliciously to distract the pope from any plan for sculpture and because they thought that Michelangelo would either refuse the commission and quarrel with the pope or that he would accept it and be less successful than Raphael, for they considered that Michelangelo's talent was for sculpture, which indeed was true. Michelangelo, who until then had not worked in colours and who knew how difficult it is to paint a ceiling, tried in every way to extricate himself. He proposed Raphael in his place and gave as an excuse that this was not his art and that he could not succeed in it, and went so far in his attempts at refusal that the pope began to grow angry and showed such obstinate determination that Michelangelo decided to undertake the work.

The tremendous task began on May 10, 1508. The first plan was simply to represent the figures of the twelve apostles in the lunettes and to fill the rest of the space with an ornamental decoration. Bramante raised a scaffolding in the chapel and several painters who had had practical experience in fresco painting were brought from Florence. We have already said that Michelangelo could only work alone. He began by declaring that Bramante's scaffolding was of no use and replaced it with one of his own invention. As for the Florentine painters who Francesco Granacci had recruited for him, Giuliano Bugiardini, Jacopo di Sandro, the elder Indaco, and Agnolo di Donnino, he took a dislike to them and sent them away. He remained alone, shut up in the chapel with a few workmen, like Giovanni Michi, and far from allowing the great difficulty of the undertaking to dampen his courage he enlarged his plan and decided to paint not only the ceiling, but the walls of the chapel down to the old frescoes.

It is dangerous to attempt to describe the "Last Judgment"; it is indeed impossible. Analyses and commentaries have been multiplied, but they kill the spirit by taking it in detail. We must face the vision squarely and lose ourselves in the abyss of that spirit. It is terrifying and, if regarded calmly, incomprehensible—it must be hated or adored. It stifles and excites; there is no nature, no landscape, no atmosphere, no tenderness, almost nothing human; the symbolism of a primitive and the science of a decadent; an architecture of naked convulsed bodies; a barren, savage and devouring thought, like a south wind over a sandy desert. There is no corner of shade, no spring to slake the thirst; it is a whirling spout of fire, the vertigo of a delirious emotion, with no goal except the God in which it loses itself. The whole calls on God, fears Him and proclaims Him. A whirlwind blows across this throng of giants—the same whirlwind which sweeps through space the God who has created the sun and hurled it like a ball of fire into the ether. There is no escape from the groaning of the tempest which surrounds and deafens you. Either you must hate this brutal force or abandon yourself to it without resistance like those souls of Dante whirled along by an eternal cyclone. When we realise that that hell was for four years the very soul of Michelangelo we understand why his life was burnt out by it and why for a long time afterward he remained like a soil exhausted by too much use and no longer productive. Above that ceiling and those vaults built up of huge bodies, where tumultous confusion and powerful unity combine to evoke the monstrous dream of a Hindu and the imperious logic and iron will of ancient Rome, there blooms a beauty that is natural and pure. There has never been anything like it. It is at once both bestial and divine, the exquisite perfume of Hellenic grace mingles with the savage odour of primitive humanity. These giants with their Olympian shoulders and huge thighs and loins wherein we feel, as the sculptor Guillaume said, "the weight of heavy entrails" are as yet hardly free from their double origin, their two progenitors, the beast and the god. A series of drawings at Oxford University shows in what springs of realism the genius of Michelangelo bathed itself and of what common clay his heroes are moulded.

On the flat part of the vault, in the centre, are the nine scenes from Genesis, Æschylean visions:[5] the divine solitude, the dreadful moment of the creation, the athletic god carried by clouds of spirits, man just rousing from

[5] The ceiling of the Sistine Chapel is rectangular in form, measuring forty metres in length by thirteen in width.

I. On the level part of the vault are nine scenes from Genesis; the Eternal dividing light from darkness, the Eternal creating the sun and moon, the Eternal dividing the waters, the Creation of man, the Creation of woman, the Temptation, Cain and Abel, the Deluge, and the Drunkenness of Noah.

II. In every angle of the imaginary frame surrounding these nine scenes is a naked figure seated on a pedestal, twenty in all. Vasari calls these the "Ignudi." Between them, and below each one of the five scenes from Genesis, is a small medallion the colour of bronze.

III. At the springing of the arches of the vault, in the twelve pendentives, twelve prophets and sibyls are seated between pilasters crowned by naked children who act as caryatids and are each accompanied by two little geniuses. The figures are Jeremiah, Ezekiel, Joel, Zachariah, Isaiah, Daniel, Jonah, the Persian, Erythræan, Cumæan, Delphian, and Libyan Sibyls.

IV. Between the prophets and sibyls, in the space above the twelve arched windows, are the precursors and ancestors of Christ, groups of two or three persons divided into two sections by an archivolt in the midst of which are written on tablets the names of the precursors. Above these triangles, on the ribs, are naked youths. Between the triangles and under the thrones of the prophets and sibyls, whose names they carry on tablets, are children's figures.

V. In the four pendentives formed by the angles of the ceiling are David, Conqueror of Goliath; Judith and Holofernes; the Brazen Serpent, and the Hanging of Haman.

the sleep of earth and regarding as an equal, face to face, the God who awakes him—both in silent readiness for the struggle—the calm and powerful woman in whom sleeps humanity—those human frames like temples of flesh and blood, torsos like trunks of trees, arms like columns and great thighs; those beings great with power and passion and crime and the results and punishments of their crimes—the Temptation, Cain and the Deluge.

At the angles of the cornice which frames these scenes are the twenty savage Ignudi, living statues, either struggling in convulsions of fear and fury or falling back, overwhelmed and exhausted—a symphony of mad force which sweeps in every direction and beats against the walls.

As gigantic supporters of the ceilings are seated in the pendentives twelve prophets and sibyls who suffer and dream; disdainful Lybica; Persica, purblind and restless; Cumæa, with huge arms and pendent breasts; the beautiful Erythræa, strong, calm and scornful; Delphica, the virgin with the lovely body and fierce eyes; Daniel, his lips compressed, his eyes fixed; Isaiah, bitter and contemptuous; Ezekiel, at war with himself and with a Genius of sombre beauty who seems to be pointing out to him the one who is to come; Jeremiah, plunged in the depths of silence, and Jonah, panting and breathless, cast out from the jaws of death—all those tragic torches of thought which burned in the night of the pagan and Jewish world; all the human knowledge which awaited the Saviour.

Above the twelve windows the Precursors and Ancestors of Christ also wait and dream in the midst of the storm. The night is long and full of evil visions. They try to sleep, they try to forget how long they must wait; they are silent and they ponder, anxious and overwhelmed. A seated woman alone dares to look squarely in the face of the menacing future. In her fixed and dilated eyes I can see that secret feeling which weighs on all these beings, a burden they dare not acknowledge—fear. At the four angles of the ceiling are displayed the sinister acts which saved the people of God—David slaying Goliath, Judith bearing the head of Holofernes, the Hebrews writhing under the bites of the serpents of Moses, and Haman crucified. Fierce barbaric stories of murderous fanaticism —a roundhead in Cromwell's time would have chosen no other subjects.

Fear, sadness, suspense. We who know how thirty years later Michelangelo completed with the Last Judgment the cycle of his idea, we know what they awaited—the Christ who comes to destroy.

Michelangelo had suffered terribly during this gigantic labour. His letters show intense discouragement which even his wonderful visions could not help. "This is not my profession," he complained. "I waste my time without any results. God help me."[6]

These were years of desperate efforts in the midst of enemies who spied upon him and hoped for his failure. He nearly gave up the work and fled again. Just as he began to paint the Deluge the whole ceiling began to grow mouldy so that the figures could hardly be distinguished. Michelangelo seized that as an excuse for giving up, but San Gallo discovered that the trouble came from the lime, which had too much water in it, and the pope ordered the artist to go on with his work.

Julius II was irritated by Michelangelo's slowness and by the fact that he persisted in hiding his work from him. There was constant friction between them.

"One day," says Condivi, "the pope asked him when he would finish and Michelangelo answered, according to his custom, 'When I can.' The pope, who was irritable, struck him with his staff, saying, 'When I can, when I

[6] Letter to his father, January 27, 1509.

can!' Michelangelo rushed home and began to make his preparations to leave Rome. Luckily the pope sent hurriedly after him an amiable young man named Accursio, who gave him five hundred ducats, soothed him as well as he could and apologised for Julius II and Michelangelo accepted the excuses. The next day, however, they began again and when the pope threatened to have him thrown from his scaffolding Michelangelo had to give way. He had the scaffolding removed and uncovered the ceiling sooner than he had intended. 'That is why,' he said, 'that that work was not carried on as far as I would have wished. The pope's impatience prevented.' "

The first part of the paintings was finished on September 1st, 1510, and the pope was able to see the four chief compositions of the ceiling before his departure for Bologna. In January and February, 1511, Michelangelo drew the cartoons for the "teste e faccie attorno di ditta capella," the pictures for the corners and the lunettes, and the second period of the work began. In August, 1511, Julius II celebrated mass in the Sistine Chapel, "ut picturas novas ibidem noviter detectas videret"; and the entire work was finished in October, 1512. On October 31, 1512, the Sistine Chapel was opened to the public.

Soon after, on February 21, 1513, Julius II died.

Chapter 3

The Failure of the Great Plans
(1513–1534)

MICHELANGELO, FREED from the Sistine Chapel, returned
to sculpture and to the great project which he had most
at heart, the tomb of Julius II.[1]

Julius II in his will had charged Cardinal d'Agen,
Lionardo Grossi della Rovere and the Prothonotary Lorenzo Pucci (later on Cardinal de Santi Quatro) to continue the enterprise. He had stipulated that the monument
should not be executed in the colossal proportions which
were originally determined on. But it does not appear that
his executors compiled with this request. Michelangelo
writes in 1524 "at the death of Pope Julius and the beginning of Leo's reign Aginensis (Cardinal d'Agen)
wished to enlarge the monument and to make the work
more considerable than was my first design and a contract
was made."

The sixth of March, 1513, Michelangelo signed what

[1] Michelangelo abandoned painting for almost twenty years and
did not take it up again until 1529.

50

was in effect a new contract by which he pledged himself
to execute the monument in seven years and not to undertake any other work of importance till it was finished.
He was to receive sixteen thousand five hundred ducats,
from which were deducted the three thousand five hundred which had been paid during the life of Julius II.[2]
The new plan included thirty-two large statues, and the
monument was to be built against the wall of the church.
"At each of the three sides were two tabernacles, both
containing a group of two figures; in front of each of the
pilasters flanking the tabernacles was to be a statue. Between the tabernacles were reliefs in bronze, on the platform above was the statue of the pope supported by four
figures and surrounded by six others on pedestals. Finally
from the platform was to rise a little sanctuary thirty-four
palms high[3] and containing five statues larger in size than
the others."[4]

For three years Michelangelo devoted himself almost
exclusively to this work and from that period of vigour
and maturity, of relative calm and satisfying accomplish-
ment, came his most perfect piece of sculpture, the Moses.
This statue, originally intended for one of the six colossal
figures crowning the upper story of the tomb, in the end
was itself the complete expression of the whole monument. The Moses is the older brother of the Prophets of
the Sistine, sprung from the same vehement and passionate inspiration, but more commanding, more sure and
more master of himself (we shall come upon him again
at the completion of the work thirty years later, for Mi-

---

[2] "I did not want them to charge me with the 3,000 crowns
which I had already received, for I showed that they owed me
much more than that. But Aginensis said to me that I was a
cheat." (Letter of Michelangelo, 1524.)

[3] Twenty-six feet three inches.

[4] Contratti, 635 ff.

chelangelo was never tired of returning to him). The two Slaves[5] now in the Louvre, who were to be placed against the pilasters of the lower story, immortal symbols of the weariness of living and of the revolt against life,—the voluptuous hero with his beautiful body overcome by deadly torpor and the athlete, vanquished but unsubdued, who writhes in his bonds, "bent like a spring," gathering himself together and hurling his scorn into the face of heaven—both belong to this period. Probably the Caryatid of the Hermitage at St. Petersburg, which was certainly meant for one of the groups of conquerors in the niches, was made at this time as well as the models for many statues.

The general subject of the monument according to Condivi and to Vasari who preserved the sayings of Michelangelo himself, was an allegory cold, abstruse and courtier-like, as we must admit the subjects of his undertakings very often were. His nature was timid and lacked independence, but fortunately the force of his passionate feeling carried everything before it. Vainly did he bind himself to lifeless and commonplace programs, vainly attempt to force himself to glorify the established order and the powers that be. At the very first step he took all false pretenses fell away and a furious cry of revolt against the baseness of the world and the bondage of life broke forth. So the statues of this monument which was to express with stale flattery that "all the virtues were prisoners of

---

[5] The two Slaves were given in 1544 by Michelangelo to Robert Strozzi, who was at that time banished from Florence and had taken refuge in France. They finally reached the Constable de Montmorency's Château of Ecouen, and Henri de Montmorency when he died in 1632 gave them to Cardinal de Richelieu. From the Château de Richelieu they were moved in the seventeenth century to the gardens of the Maréchal de Richelieu in Paris. It is thanks to Lenoir that they were preserved to France in 1793.

death now that the pope was dead" became, unconsciously perhaps to their creator, hymns of heroic scorn and expressions of moral grandeur crushed by force yet rising unconquered.

But the peculiar quality of these figures compared with the work which was to follow is that they preserve in all their passionate agony a balance and a certain melancholy serenity which the artist of the tombs of the Medici no longer possessed.[6]

In that serene and fruitful period, while the excitement of his work in the Sistine Chapel quieted little by little, like the calming of a stormy sea, Michelangelo seems to have accepted only one other commission, that for the Christ of the Minerva which came from three Romans, Bernardo Cencio, Mario Scapucci and Metello Varj. Yet beginning with the summer of 1515 his letters show that he feared and foresaw the interruption of his work.

---

[6] Condivi wrote that according to Michelangelo the statues of the bound men which were to be placed against the pilasters of the lower part of the tomb "represented the liberal arts, painting, sculpture and architecture each with its characteristic attributes, in such a way that they could be easily recognised. At the same time they expressed the idea that all the virtues were prisoners of death with Pope Julius and that they would never find anyone to encourage them and to support them as he had done."

Some sketches at Oxford show a number of these prisoners struggling against their chains. The large statues of the upper story were to personify St. Paul, Moses, Adam, Life and Contemplation; Julius II was represented asleep on an open sarcophagus which was supported by two angels, "one smiling to express the joy of heaven, and the other weeping to represent the sorrow of earth."

A large pen-and-ink drawing in the Uffizi partly shows the architecture of the monument—that Charles Garnier called the architecture of a goldsmith—and which is indeed a frame to group the sculptured figures together as well as possible. I would like to believe that this drawing refers not to the plan of 1513, but to the simplified plan of 1516.

"I must make a great effort this summer," he writes on June 16 to his brother Buonarroto, "to bring my work rapidly to an end, for I think that I shall soon have to enter the service of the pope."

The new pope, Leo X (Giovanni Medici), at first left Michelangelo entirely free. He was so anxious to gain the hearts of his former adversaries that he took very good care not to seem to put any obstacle in the way of the glorification of his predecessor. He soon found, however, that the tomb absorbed Michelangelo's energies completely and he decided to draw him away from it in order to devote him to the service of his own house. He planned to build the facade of S. Lorenzo, the church of the Medici in Florence. Several artists, Baccio d'Agnolo, Antonio da San Gallo, Andrea and Jacopo Sansovino and Raphael himself brought their plans to him during his stay in Florence in November and December, 1515. But whether because Raphael was kept in Rome by his post of superintendent of the construction of St. Peter's in which he had lately succeeded the old Giuliano da San Gallo in August, 1515, or whether Leo X wished to attach to himself Michelangelo—whose family pride he had already flattered by naming his brother Buonarroto *Comes Palatinus* and by giving the Buonarroti the right to place in their arms the "palla" of the Medici with their lilies and the monogram of the pope—at any rate it was to him that Leo X turned. Michelangelo, stirred by the growing fame of Raphael, allowed himself to be drawn into this new task which it was physically impossible for him to accomplish without neglecting the old one and which was to cause him endless worry and vexation. His correspondence with Domenico Buoninsegni shows plainly that he tried to deceive himself into thinking that he could carry on the two undertakings simultaneously.

The heirs of Juius II, however, were more clear-sighted and in order to fight fire with fire they tried to bind him by a third contract on July 8, 1516. By this agreement the monument of the pope was to be diminished by one-half and the number of the statues reduced from thirty-two to twenty. They gave Michelangelo nine years more in which to complete the work, with full liberty to execute it in Florence, Pisa or Carrara. In return they forced from him the formal agreement that he would not undertake any other important work "opus saltim magni momenti." That clause was aimed directly at the plans of Leo X. Michelangelo signed this in good faith, for he thought that it would not prevent his making some statues for the facade of S. Lorenzo. His imagination carried him away. He was more and more attracted by Leo's project and he let himself go so far as to write that he would undertake the work and he sent a design for the façade. Then, almost at once, he was seized with scruples and wanted to rid himself of the greater part of the task by turning it over to the architect Baccio d'Agnolo and only reserving for himself the principal statues. The pope agreed to everything, sure of what would happen, for it was no secret that Michelangelo was incapable of collaborating with anyone, no matter who he might be. As a matter of fact Michelangelo was not satisfied with the model of the façade which Baccio made according to his plan. He made another one, and in the end grew irritated with Baccio, whom he accused of having an understanding with his enemies. Little by little his enthusiasm for the work grew.

He wrote restlessly to Domenico Buoninsegni in July, 1517: "I wish to make of this façade of S. Lorenzo a work which shall be a mirror of architecture and of sculpture for all Italy. The pope and the cardinal[7] must

---

[7] Cardinal Giulio Medici, future Clement VII.

make up their minds quickly whether they want me to do it or not. If they want me to do it they must sign a contract and give me full powers. I will finish it in six years. Messer Domenico, give me an exact answer as to the intentions of the pope and the cardinal. That would afford me the greatest satisfaction."

Here it is Michelangelo himself who begs Leo X to give him this heavy burden, who trembles for fear of not getting it, and is consumed with the desire to bind himself to a new servitude! Januray 19, 1518, he signed a contract with Leo X by which he agreed to erect the façade of S. Lorenzo in eight years.

It was to be composed of:

First: An inferior order of eight fluted columns, eleven brasses[8] high, three portals with four statues five brasses high and seven bas-reliefs; and around the sides on each lateral face two columns, and between them a figure in high relief.

Second: A superior order of eight pilasters from six to seven brasses high; on the façade four seated bronze statues; and on each side two pilasters and a statue.

Third: The upper cornice carrying an entablature of eight pilasters in front and two on the side, with four niches in the façade, and one on each side intended for six marble statues five and a half brasses high.

There were besides on the façade, undoubtedly in the lower story, seven bas-reliefs of marble with life-size subjects, five squares and two round plaques. In the centre a pediment with the arms of the Medici.

Michelangelo had the choice of executing the work himself or of having it done after his models. The heirs of Julius II were obliged to give way to the order of Leo X and to be satisfied with the permission which he gave to

[8] A brasse is 1.62 metres.

Michelangelo still to go on with the work on the monument of Julius in Florence. Even that permission was very soon withdrawn, according to Michelangelo. "Pope Leo," he writes, "does not want me to do the monument of Julius." When he began to work on it again in his atelier in Florence he says: "The Medici, who later on became Pope Clement and who was then in Florence, saw that I was working at the tomb and he would no longer permit it. For that reason I was prevented from doing anything until the Medici became pope."

Michelangelo always sought excuses for not finishing his undertakings. The real culprit was his eager and changeable genius, uncontrollable and constantly seized with enthusiasm for some new idea. He no more succeeded in raising the façade of S. Lorenzo than in finishing the tomb.

His terrible mania for doing everything himself drove him—insteading of staying and working in Florence—into going to Carrara to oversee the quarrying of the blocks of marble. There he found himself in all sorts of difficulties. The Medici wanted to use the quarries of Pietra Santa, which had been lately bought by Florence, instead of those of Carrara and Michelangelo, because he took sides with the Carrarese, found himself suspected by the Cardinal Giulio de' Medici of having been bought by them; and because he was forced in the end to obey the strict orders of the pope he was persecuted by the people of Carrara, who made an arrangement with the Genoese boatmen at Pisa so that he could not secure any barge to transport his marble. He had to build a road several miles in length across the mountains with pick and shovel. The ill-will of the people of Pietra Santa and the stupidity of the workmen who did not understand their work so upset him that he fell ill at Seravezza from overstrain and worry. He felt that his vigour, his health and his ideas were being wasted in this life of an engineer and contractor. He was dying with impatience to begin the façade, but the blocks of marble did not reach Florence because the barges were stopped or the Arno was dry. They arrived at last and the marble was unloaded, but instead of setting to work Michelangelo returned to Seravezza and Pietra Santa. He was obstinately determined not to begin until he had gathered in Florence, just as he had done before in Rome for the tomb of Julius II, all the material which would be necessary for the entire undertaking, a veritable mountain of marble. He kept putting off the moment of beginning. Was it not the truth—though he did not admit it even to himself—that he was really afraid of the great architectural undertaking into which he had imprudently plunged and for which he had so little training? How, indeed, could he have acquired this new art which he had had no chance of practising? Had he not promised too much and did he not feel himself in a blind alley with no way out, where he no longer dared either to advance or retreat?

All his efforts were unsuccessful, even those for the transportation of the marble. He was cheated by his workmen, and four of the six monolithic columns sent to Florence were shattered on the way, one of them at Florence itself. At last the pope and Cardinal de' Medici grew impatient at this useless loss of so much precious time in the marshes and quarries of Pietra Santa and on March 10, 1520, an order of the pope clearly and completely released Michelangelo from the agreement of 1518 concerning the façade of S. Lorenzo and from all obligations in regard to it. Michelangelo only knew of this through the arrival at Seravezza of the gangs of workmen sent by Cardinal Giulio to take his place. He was cruelly hurt.

"I do not begrudge the cardinal," he says, "the three

years which I have lost here. I do not blame him because I am exhausted by this work for S. Lorenzo. I do not blame him for the great affront of having ordered me to do this work and then of taking it away from me—I do not even know for what reason. I do not count against him all that I have spent, which amounts to this: Pope Leo takes back the quarry with the blocks already cut; I have left the money that I have in hand—500 ducats—and I am given my liberty."

He could not hold his patrons responsible. The fault was his own, as he well knew, and that was his worst punishment. Justi has said, not unreasonably, that he committed the sin against the Holy Ghost in wasting so many years in such unimportant work. What did he accomplish from 1515 to 1520 in the fulness of his vigour? Plans which he could never carry out, plans for the façade of S. Lorenzo, plans for the tomb of Julius II, plans for the tomb of Dante, whose remains the Academicians of Florence wanted to bring back from Ravenna to his own country[9]—for in October, 1519, in the midst of the very worst of his difficulties he had not hesitated to offer his services to Leo X to "raise to the divine poet a monument worthy of him."

One single work was realised amidst all these dreams: the Christ of the Minerva, and it is the coldest and dullest thing he ever did—a work of Michelangelo (and this is almost unbelievable) which is commonplace and uninspiring. It can hardly even be called his, for he did not finish it himself, but gave it over to the neglect of his assistant, Pietro Urbano, a bungler without talent and incurably lazy, who, when he was ordered to accompany

[9] Appeal of the Academicians of Florence to Leo X, signed by Michelangelo. (Gotti, Vol. II, p. 84.)

the statue to Rome and to finish it, ruined it by his awkwardness and left it there hopelessly marred.[10]

Cardinal Giulio de' Medici, when he had extricated Michelangelo from this hopeless enterprise, determined to turn his genius in a new direction and one in which he could direct him more closely. He entrusted him with the construction of the new sacristy of S. Lorenzo and the tombs of the Medici. In November, 1520, Michelangelo submitted to him a drawing which met with his approval. This original plan was for four tombs: those of Lorenzo the Magnificent, Giuliano his brother, his son Giuliano, Duke of Nemours, and his grandson Lorenzo, Duke of Urbino. The work was begun before April, 1521, but was not pushed vigorously until after the nomination on No-

[10] Michelangelo ended his work in April, 1520. The Christ was sent to Rome in March, 1521. Pietro Urbano worked at it from June until the middle of August when he suddenly left Rome.

Sebastiano del Piombo writes to Michelangelo in September, 1521: "Pietro Urbano has mutilated everything. In particular he has shortened the right foot and you can see clearly that he has cut off the toes: he has even shortened the fingers, especially those of the right hand which held the cross. Frizzi says that they look as if they had been made by a 'baker.' That hand does not even look like marble; you would think it had been made by a pastry cook, so stiff are the fingers. You can see, too, that he has worked at the beard and you would think he had modelled it with a blunt knife. He has also mutilated one of the nostrils, and almost spoilt the nose."

Michelangelo had to commission the sculptor, Federigo Frizzi, to finish the work. With his customary honesty he offered to make an entirely new statue for Metello Varj, who had ordered the work from him, but Varj declined. Michelangelo was so ashamed of the Christ of the Minerva that when the statue was unveiled in December, 1521, Lionardo Sellajo, one of his friends in Rome, took great care that everyone should know that it was not by Michelangelo, but that he had simply retouched it.

vember 19, 1522, of Cardinal Giulio de' Medici to the pontifical throne under the name of Clement VII.[11]

In May, 1524, Clement VII accepted the idea, suggested to him by the flattering Salviati, of adding to the four sarcophagi already planned tombs for Leo X and for himself and of giving them the place of honour. In June Michelangelo sent him a new plan as well as the drawings for the Library of S. Lorenzo, the building of which had also been entrusted to him.

Clement VII wished to monopolise Michelangelo's services, and he suggested to him in January, 1524, that he should join the order of the Franciscans so that he might be given a benefice. Michelangelo refused to do this, but the pope decided, nevertheless, to allow him a monthly pension of three times the amount for which he had asked[12] and a house in the neighbourhood of S. Lorenzo. Everything seemed to be going well and the work on the chapel was progressing when Michelangelo suddenly left the house which had been given to him and refused to accept Clement VII's pension. He was going through another crisis of discouragement and doubt. The heirs of Julius II could not forgive him for having abandoned the work that he had undertaken. They accused him of unfaithfulness and threatened him with the law. He was terrified at the idea of a lawsuit, for his conscience told him that his adversaries were in the right, and he was tormented by the thought that he had not kept his word.

---

[11] After the death of Leo X on December 1, 1521, and during all the pontificate of Adrian VI, who died on September 23, 1523, Cardinal Giulio de' Medici had put a "mute" on all his undertakings. It is probable that during that year's respite (1522–23) Michelangelo was able to take up again the tomb of Julius II, and that he worked at the admirable Victory of the Bargello and at the scarcely blocked-in figures of the Boboli Grotto.

[12] Fifty crowns. Michelangelo only asked for fifteen.

He felt that he could not accept the money of Clement VII as long as he had not yet either given back that of Julius II or carried out his promises. But struggle as he would he lacked strength to free himself from the ties which bound him to the pope, and necessity forced him to take the pension which he had refused. He continued to protest while he worked. By the end of October, 1525, he had only blocked out four figures, the allegories of the seasons. He was always thinking of the monument of Julius II and he tried to simplify his plan by changing it to a tomb built against the wall, like those of Pius II and Pius III at St. Peter's. He felt that he could finish the figures within a stated time and then give to Pope Clement all the rest of his powers, "and in truth they are feeble, for I am old and ought not to have all these worries, for they affect me greatly. You can not work while your hands are doing one thing and your head another, especially in sculpture."[13]

Clement VII seemed at times to be touched by Michelangelo's troubles and expressed an affectionate interest in him and his work. He sent him a letter on December 23, 1525, in which he said:

"You know that popes do not have long lives and we could not long more ardently than we do to see the chapel with the tombs of our family and to know that it is finished and also the Library. We recommend them both to your zeal. Nevertheless we are trying to possess ourselves in salutary patience and we pray God that He may inspire you to carry on all these works at once. Do not fear that

[13] He was fifty years old. In 1517, when he was forty-two, in a letter to Domenico Buoninsegni he called himself "old." In 1523 in a letter to Cardinal Domenico Grimani, he emphasised the lessening of his strength through age. "If I work a day," he says, "I must rest for four."

you will ever lack either work or rewards as long as we live. Go on with God and our blessing."

But the incurable frivolity of the Medici regained the upper hand, and instead of relieving Michelangelo of part of his work he laid new burdens on him; a Ciborium for S. Lorenzo and a ridiculous Colossus which it was proposed to put up outside the Medici gardens, the fantastic plans for which took up much of Michelangelo's time.[14]

It is sad to see this poor great man trying so hard to understand the absurd whims of his Mæcenas that he ends by almost becoming interested in them.

"I have thought about the Colossus," he writes to Fattucci in the autumn of 1525; "I have indeed thought a great deal about it. It seems to me that it would not be well placed outside the Medici gardens because it would take up too much room in the street. A better place, I think, would be where the barber's shop is. There it would not be so much in the way. As for the expenses of expropriation, I think to reduce them we could make the figure seated, and as it could be hollow the shop could be placed inside so the rent would not be lost. It seems to me a good idea to put in the hand of the Colossus a horn of abun-

---

[14] Thode pretends that Michelangelo did not take this seriously and that the letter which follows is "ironisch und humorvolle." Full of humor, yes, but do not think it ironical. If there is any trace of irony it is rather on the side of the pope, who might have been making fun of Michelangelo's naïveté and of his well-known tendency to grow enthusiastic over any new undertaking, particularly the most fantastic ones. In fact after frequent exchanges of letters in October and November, 1525, Fattucci, a friend of Michelangelo, warned him secretly in December that "the Colossus was only a joke." Michelangelo had not suspected any malice in this scheme and had already pictured in his mind the bizarre Colossus to which he gave a frankly popular character, monstrous and comic, like one of Aristo's giants.

dance, and this could be hollow and would serve as a chimney. The head could also be made use of, I should think, for the poultryman, my very good friend who lives on the square, said to me secretly that it would make a wonderful dovecote. I have another and still better idea—but in that case the statue must be made very much larger, which would not be impossible, for towers are made with stone—and that is that the head should serve as a bell-tower to S. Lorenzo, which now has none. By placing the bell so that the sound would come out of the mouth it would seem as if the giant cried for mercy, especially on holidays when they use the big bells."

Michelangelo had constant trouble with his workmen, and to these worries and his pangs of conscience were added domestic difficulties which never ceased to embitter his life. During the period of the Sistine frescoes it was his relations with his brothers that gave him most trouble, for they tried to make use of him and he had to watch them sharply. Then it was his father whom he adored with almost religious reverence and who undoubtedly loved him, but who, irritable like himself, and peevish and suspicious, picked unfair quarrels and spread odious calumnies about him.

In the midst of all these difficulties the work did not progress at all. A letter of June, 1526, says that one statue of a captain had been begun, as well as four allegories and the Madonna, but as a matter of fact not one of these was ready in 1527. As for the Library and the Medici Chapel they were hardly begun.

At this moment the revolution broke out in Florence (April, 1527).

Michelangelo had until then shown in politics the same indecision from which he had suffered so much in his own affairs and even in his art. He never succeeded in reconciling his love of liberty with his obligations to the Medici.

It must be admitted that this violent genius was always timid in action; he never incurred any risk through struggling against the powers of this world on political or religious grounds. He was afraid of compromising himself. He was afraid of everything. He was always afraid. If in spite of his natural timidity he let himself be drawn into the Florentine Revolution of 1527 he must have been driven by deep despair and the belief that his life was practically lost. That extremity of suffering brought to the surface and into action his fundamental beliefs.

His timid introspective soul was secretly ardently republican. We can see this in the violent discussions which he had in 1545 with intimate friends, Luigi del Riccio, Antonio Petreo and Donato Giannotti, who made note of them in his "Dialogues on Dante's Divine Comedy." In these talks he defends tyrannicide with enthusiasm.

He found himself in the front ranks of the Florentine revolutionists in those days of national and republican revival which, in Florence, followed the news of the taking of Rome by the Imperialists (May 6, 1527) and the driving out of Ippolito and Alessandro de' Medici (May 17th). At first the Republic seems only to have given him artistic commissions. He was ordered to cut from a block of marble a colossal group of two figures as a companion-piece to the David. He obeyed, and began a Hercules and Cacus;[15] then changed his plan and made a sketch for a Samson slaying the Philistines. But the situation grew tragic and he was called to more pressing tasks. In October, 1528, at San Miniato he took part in a council presided over by the Gonfalonier Niccolo Capponi to discuss the question of the fortification of the town. Florence had

[15] The block of marble abandoned by Michelangelo was taken a little while afterward by his jealous rival, Bandinelli, who made from it a Hercules and Cacus which to-day still stands on the Piazza della Signoria.

summoned the architect Sebastiano Serlio and the engineer Pierfrancesco d'Urbino and had sent Francesco da San Gallo and Amadio d'Alberto to examine the fortifications of Prato, Pistoia, Pisa and Livorno. Michelangelo was chosen in his turn on January 10, 1529, in the *Collegium* of the *Nove di Milizzia* to direct the works of defense. He was named on April 6th for one year *Governatore Generale* and *Procuratore* of the fortifications of Florence, and was given a salary of one golden ducat a day.[16] He realised that the important point of defense was San Miniato for, "if the enemy gained possession of that hill they would be master of the city." He determined, therefore, to strengthen that position with bastions, but he encountered the ill-will of the Gonfalonier Capponi, who tried to send him away from Florence on various missions.

In June, 1529, he was ordered to inspect the citadel of Pisa and the fortifications of Arezzo and Livorno. In July and August he was sent to Ferrara to examine the celebrated defensive works there and to consult with the Duke, a great expert in fortifications. The Duke received him with great honour and took him over the fortifications himself, showed him his art collection and asked him for one of his works.[17] But Michelangelo suspected Capponi and the party of the Medici of taking advantage of his absence to delay the fortification of the town and his suspicions were confirmed by the neglected condition in which he found the work on his return. To block these intrigues he installed himself at San Miniato and would not stir from there again. His restless spirit felt the least breath of the rumours of treason which, as always, circu-

---

[16] Until then Michelangelo had given his services gratuitously to his country.

[17] It was for him that Michelangelo some time after this made his painting of Leda, but he never sent it to him because of some discourtesy on the part of the Ferrarese ambassador.

lated in a besieged town and which unhappily, as the future showed, were only too well founded.

Capponi, under suspicion, had been replaced as Gonfalonier by Francesco Carducci, but the untrustworthy Malatesta Baglioni, who later on was to give up the town, was named *Condottiere* and governor-general of the Florentine troops. Michelangelo foresaw his treason and confided his suspicions to Carducci. Malatesta did not fail to hear of this denunciation. He was all-powerful at Florence as Generalissimo, and since a man of his type would stop at nothing when it was a question of revenge or of the removal of a dangerous adversary, Michelangelo believed himself lost. "I had resolved, however, to await without fear the end of the war," he writes on September 25, 1529, to Battista della Palla. "But on Tuesday morning the twenty-first of September a certain man came to me outside of the Porta San Niccolo, where I was on the bastions, and whispered in my ear that if I wished to save my life I must not stay any longer in Florence. He went with me to my house, brought me some horses, and did not leave me again until he had put me outside of Florence."

Varchi, filling in the details, gives the name of the Councellor Rinaldo Corsini[18] and adds that Michelangelo had sewed twelve thousand golden florins into three quilted shirts, and that it was not without difficulty that he escaped from Florence with Rinaldo and his pupil Antonio Mini by the gate of Justice, which was the least guarded. That was on the morning of September 21st. He went through Ferrara without stopping there and arrived at Venice on September 25th. The Signory at once sent two gentlemen to do anything for him which he might

---

[18] Michelangelo does not name him, undoubtedly so as not to compromise him.

need (a proof of the fame which he enjoyed already throughout the whole of Italy). Michelangelo, however, refused everything and withdrew to the Giudecca. He thought of going to France and spoke of this intention to Battista della Palla, the agent of Francis I in Italy for the purchase of works of art. Lazare de Baïf, the ambassador of France at Venice, was told of this and wrote immediately to Francis I and to the Constable de Montmorency, urging them to profit by this chance to secure Michelangelo. The King at once offered Michelangelo a pension and a house, but by the time the letter arrived at Venice he had already returned to Florence.

His flight had caused a great sensation there. The Signory on September 30th decreed that all those who had deserted should be declared rebel and banished if they did not return by October 7th. On the date fixed Michelangelo had not returned. A decree declared the fugitives rebels and their goods confiscated, but the name of Michelangelo did not figure on the list. They gave him another chance. A few days later the Florentine envoy at Ferrara, Galeotto Guigni, informed the Signory that Michelangelo had heard of the decree too late and that he was ready to return if he would be pardoned. The Signory promised to forgive him and had a safe conduct sent to him in Venice by the stone-cutter, Bastiano di Francesco, who brought him at the same time letters from ten of his friends all beseeching him to return to Florence. He had had time to reflect on what he had done and was ashamed of his pitiful panic. He went back to Florence on November 20, 1529, and on the 23rd the decree of banishment was removed by the Signory, but the Grand Council was closed to him for three years. According to a letter of Sebastiano del Piombo, Michelangelo also had to pay to the city a fine of fifteen hundred ducats.

From that time on he did his duty bravely. He took his

place again at San Miniato, which the enemy had been bombarding for a month. He had the hill fortified all over again, and it is said that he saved the campanile by covering it with bales of wool and mattresses hung on cords. The last record of his activity during the siege is a note of February 22, 1530, which shows him climbing the dome of the cathedral, doubtless to watch the movements of the enemy or to examine into the condition of the dome itself, strained by the bombardment.

The misfortune which he had foreseen took place on August 2, 1530, when Malatesta Baglioni turned traitor. On the 12th Florence capitulated, and the Emperor turned the town over to the representative of the pope, Baccio Valori. Then the executions began. During the first few days nothing checked the vengeance of the conquerors and some of Michelangelo's best friends were among the victims. Michelangelo hid himself, it is said, in the tower of S. Niccolò oltr' Arno. He had especial reason to fear because the report had been spread that he had wished to tear down the palace of the Medici. "When the wrath of Clement VII had subsided," says Condivi, "he wrote to Florence that Michelangelo should be searched for. He added that if he was found and was willing to go on working at the tombs of the Medici he should be treated with all the consideration he deserved." Michelangelo came out of his hiding-place and in September or October, 1530, again undertook his work for the glory of those against whom he had fought.

It was not the glory of the Medici he wrought, but his own sorrow and wrath. The same thing happened here as with the tomb of Julius II. Michelangelo did not have the force to refuse a task unworthy of him: his genius was heroic, his will not so at all. He accepted the order, he even outlined a program whose sychophantic affection arouses a feeling of sadness and a pity for the humiliation of so great a man, forced to lie. A note in his own hand at the Casa Buonarroti explains one of the monuments in the following way.

"Day and Night talk together and say: In our rapid flight we have brought Duke Giuliano to death. It is therefore just that he should avenge himself. His vengeance, now that we have killed him, is to snatch away the light from us; by closing his eyes, he has closed ours, which will no longer illumine the earth. What would he have done with us if he had remained alive?"

Is not that insipid interpretation the veil of prudence which he wrapped about his rebel spirit? How much of this is really left in the work? Who can find it there? Who thinks only of the Medici before this tragic expression of a lonely and despairing soul? The burning and mighty spirit of the Sistine breathes again, and austere forms rise from the shade. Yet here everything is sadder; a funereal silence reigns. It is no longer the tragic struggle of the Son of Man. It is the void which weighs on these giants who groan and complain and on those two sombre, pondering heroes. The superb imperfection of some of these colossal figures, from which the sculptor has only torn aside with his chisel part of the veil of marble that covers them, adds still more to the impression of mysterious terror expressed by these classic divinities, half released from chaos and soon to exhaust themselves in a vain struggle against the forces of destruction. Action, resigned and powerless, turns his head aside. At his feet Day in fierce contempt for all things, shows for a moment over his shoulder, his face wrapped in clouds. He turns his back on life and plunges into passionate isolation. Night, overcome by leaden sleep and burning with fever, sinks into the midst of a stifling nightmare, like a stone into a gulf.

Thought, self-divining, bends toward the tomb his austere face bathed in shadow and considers the succession of his days. Dawn, so beautiful and pure, wakened against her will, weary of living and exhausted, stirs in mortal pain; Twilight, with bended brow, bitter and disabused, remembers the past without regret. The dolorous and resigned Virgin looks on at this threnody of negation while the child God, famished, gnaws her breast in anger.[19]

It was in this outburst of despair that Michelangelo drowned his shame at raising this monument of slavery.[20] He fell ill from overexcitement and Clement VII at-

[19] In entering the chapel of S. Lorenzo the tomb of Giuliano, Duke of Nemours, (Action) is on the right; and on the left that of Lorenzo, Duke of Urbino (the Thinker); and opposite the altar, the Virgin nursing the Child. Each of the two captains is placed in a rectangular niche flanked by two other niches which are empty. Below each of them on the fluted cover of a sarcophagus are two allegorical figures half reclining (Day and Night— Dawn and Twilight) with their backs turned. The sarcophagi are designedly much too small; there is hardly room for the figures on them. No doubt Michelangelo wished to emphasise the impression of heroic and agonising effort produced by the sight of these athletic forms turned back upon themselves in involved and constrained positions. The two tombs were finished in 1531. We know the admirable verses which Michelangelo wrote on his figure of Night and which undoubtedly date from a dozen years later, March, 1544. See Frey CIX, pp. 16–17.

[20] At this same time by a savage and instinctive reaction of his nature against the Christian pessimism by which it was stifled, Michelangelo executed some works of daring paganism like the painting of Leda caressed by the Swan (1529–1530) which, originally made for the Duke of Ferrara, was given by Michelangelo to his pupil Antonio Mini, who carried it to France, where it is said to have been destroyed about 1643 by Sublet des Noyers because of its licentiousness. A little later Michelangelo painted for Bart. Bettini a cartoon of Venus caressed by Love from which Pontormo made a picture now in the Uffizi. Other drawings full of a grandiose and severe shamelessness are probably of the same period. To the first months of the siege belongs also the admirable unfinished statue of the Apollo of the Museo Nazionale which he made for Baccio Valori in the autumn of 1530.

tempted in vain to soothe him. He sent affectionate messages to him by his secretary, Pier Paolo Marzo, urging him not to overexert himself, to work reasonably and at his leisure, to take a walk occasionally, and "not to reduce himself to the condition of a drudge." In the autumn of 1534 his life was in danger. Giovanni Battista di Paolo Mini wrote on September 29th to Valori, "Michelangelo is worn and emaciated. I have spoken of it to Bugiardino and Antonio Mini; we agreed that he had not long to live unless someone looks out for him."

Clement VII was disturbed and on November 21, 1531, by a special letter he forbade Michelangelo under pain of excommunication "to work in any way whatever, except on the tomb of Julius II and the undertaking which we have entrusted to you (ne aliquo modo laborare debeas nisi in sepulture et opera nostra quam tibi comisimus) so that you may still bring glory to Rome, your family and yourself."

He protected Michelangelo against the importunities of those who came to beg for works of art, and he reprimanded him paternally for accepting these orders. "When anyone asks you for a painting," he said, "you should fasten a brush to your foot, make four strokes and say, 'The picture is done.'" He promised also to arrange Michelangelo's difficulties with the heirs of Julius II.

On April 29, 1532, by his mediation a fourth contract was agreed upon between the representative of the heir to Julius II, the Duke of Urbino, Francesco Maria della Rovere and Michelangelo. Michelangelo promised to make a new model of the tomb, to deliver the six statues already begun and still unfinished, as well as everything else that was ready; to complete it in the course of three years at S. Pietro in Vinculi and to pay all the expenses as well as two thousand ducats in compensation for the sums which he had already received. The pope gave him permission to come for two months every year to Rome for this work. Michelangelo was agreeing to the ruin of the greatest undertaking of his life and he had besides to pay so much that he was forced to sell houses and goods.

Like the plans for Julius II, the plans for the Medici collapsed. Clement VII died on September 28, 1538. Michelangelo was at that time away from Florence and he never went back there. Duke Alessandro de' Medici hated him, and only his fear of the pope prevented the tyrant from assassinating him. Michelangelo therefore left Florence (where his brother Buonarroto died in January, 1534) just after he had lost his father, Lodovico, in June of that same year. Nothing bound him any longer to his own country, and he was never to see it again.

That was the end of the chapel of the Medici. It was never completed.[21] What we know of it to-day is only a very far-away suggestion of what he had dreamed. Barely the lifeless skeleton of the architectural decoration is left. Michelangelo had only made (partially) seven statues— Lorenzo da Urbino, Giuliano de Nemours, the four allegorical figures and the Madonna—and he had barely begun some of the others which were planned; he had abandoned to Raffaeli da Montelupo and Giovanni Montorsoli the figures of S. Cosmo and S. Damien for the tomb of Lorenzo the Magnificent and to Tribolo the figures for the tomb of Giuliano the brother of Lorenzo,

[21] In the plan of construction (a square crowned by a dome with fluted pilasters and niches with pediments) Michelangelo was influenced by Brunelleschi and Vitruvius, whom he was studying at that time. There was very little ornamentation and the idea of the plan was clear, simple and abstract. With Michelangelo, architecture is always a frame for his statues. He even went so far as to write, in 1560, to Cardinal Carpi that the divisions of architecture were the same as those of the human frame, and no one who was not "un buon maestro di figure" and did not understand anatomy could be an architect.

which were to represent the Earth crowned with cypress, her head bowed, weeping, and Heaven with lifted arms, radiant with joy. When these statues were ready to be placed no one knew where they should go. Vasari inquired in vain of Michelangelo in 1562 what statues he had intended for the empty niches beside the captains, above the doors and in the pavilions at the corners and "what sort of painting he had planned for the walls." Evidently the Medici Chapel, so bare and cold to-day, was to have had a complete decoration of painting and sculpture of which it is impossible for us to form any idea.

Almost the same thing is true of the Laurentian Library. Michelangelo never took any interest in it except in 1525–1526, when the pope wanted him to write about it almost every week. When he left Florence he had only completed the construction of the vestibule and the ceiling of the chief structure. The staircase had not been begun. When the Grand Duke Cosmo wished to have it finished by Tribolo in 1558 no model of Michelangelo's could be found. Vasari begged him to say what his plan had been and Michelangelo answered that he would tell him willingly if he could remember it, but he had only a vague idea, as if in a dream, of a certain staircase, but he did not think it could be the one he had planned, because it was absurd.[22]

---

[22] He sent a model in 1559. It is from this model that Vasari executed the much-criticised staircase of the Laurentian. In spite of faults it shows the rugged genius of Michelangelo, who seemed to enjoy making difficulties for himself. That breakneck staircase, conceived in such a dry, hard and complicated way, but strong and violent, and which ever seeks to accentuate the ascending lines, is certainly a product of the same spirit which created the Medici tombs. Besides it is well to note that the faults were emphasised by the manner in which Vasari carried it out. Michelangelo had recommended that the staircase be made of wood, but Cosmo held to the idea of building it in stone.

He had so completely given up all these undertakings that he had wiped them from his memory, or rather his memory had disappeared with them.

"Memory and mind have gone on ahead," he wrote, "to wait for me in the other world."

Chapter 4

Vittoria Colonna (1535–1547)

MICHELANGELO, WORN OUT and discouraged, returned definitely to Rome on September 23, 1534, and there he remained until his death. He was in a condition of great mental unrest, his heart hungry for love. This was the period of those strange violent and mystical passions for beautiful young men like Gherardo Perini, Febo di Poggio and, most loved of all and most worthily so, Tommaso dei Cavalieri. These attachments, about which most historians have preferred to be silent, were an almost religious delirium of love for the divinity of beauty and hold an important place in the work of Michelangelo. It is to their inspiration that most of his love-poems are due. For a long time this was either not known or a stupid and unfortunate attempt was made to conceal it. Even in 1623 Michelangelo's grandnephew in his first edition of the "Rime" did not dare publish the poems to Tommaso dei Cavalieri with their real titles, but dedicated them to a woman. This error persisted until Cæsare Guasti, in his edition of 1863, re-established the exact text, but nevertheless did not dare admit that Tommaso dei Cavalieri was a real person and forced himself to believe that Vittoria Colonna was concealed under the fictitious name. Mezières in his "L'Œuvre et la Vie de Michelange," published in 1876, repeated this same mistake, which was only finally denounced and corrected by Scheffler and Symonds in 1878.

Tommaso dei Cavalieri, according to Vasari and Varchi, was "a young Roman gentleman, devoted to art and of incomparable personal beauty," whom Michelangelo met in the autumn of 1532. It is in 1533–1534 that this friendship reached its height and inspired his most ardent poems and letters. Cavalieri remained a faithful friend to Michelangelo to his very last hour, at which indeed he was present. He made use of this friendship only for the good of his friend. Not only did he take devoted care of the old man in his last years, but he saw to the carrying out of his wishes while he was alive and after his death. It was he who persuaded him to complete the wooden model of the dome of St. Peter's and who preserved his plans for the construction of the Capitol. Their names would always be associated together even if his beauty had not inspired some of Michelangelo's most perfect sonnets.[1]

[1] See in the edition of Michelangelo's poems by Carl Frey, "Die Dichtungen des Michelangelo Buonarroti," Berlin, 1897, the sonnets, CIX, LXXVI, XLV, etc.

Vasari tells us that Michelangelo made a life-size drawing of Cavalieri, the only portrait which he ever made, for he had a horror of copying a living person unless they were of incomparable beauty.

He adds that he made him beautiful presents, "many astonishing drawings, a Ganymede carried to Heaven by the eagle of Zeus, a Tityos with the vulture feeding on his heart, the fall of Phaeton and the chariot of the Sun into the Po, and a Bacchanale of children—all works of the rarest beauty and of such perfection that their like has never been seen."

All these attachments, however, were to be eclipsed by his friendship with Vittoria Colonna. She was the daughter of Fabrizio Colonna, Lord of Paliano, Prince of Tagliacozzo, and of Agnesena di Montefeltro, daughter of the great Federigo, Duke of Urbino. She had married Ferrante Francesco d'Avalos, Marquis di Pescara, the victor of Pavia, who treated her badly, but whom she loved. A widow since 1525, she had turned for consolation to religion and poetry. Her sonnets, in which she sang her idealised love, had been well known throughout Italy since 1530 and had won for her a fame unique among the women of her day. She was a friend of all the great poets and great writers: Bembo, Castiglione who entrusted to her the manuscript of his "Cortegiano," Ariosto who celebrated her in his Orlando, Paul Jove, Bernardo Tasso and Ludovico Dolce. But after 1534 religion absorbed her and she was carried away by the movement for the reform and regeneration of the Catholic Church. Although she was a friend of all the men who personified in Italy this spirit of religious freedom, Cardinal Contarini and Cardinal Pole, Giberti, Sadolet, Bernadino Ochino, Pietro Carnesecchi, and in touch with Renée of Ferrara and Marguerite of Navarre, yet she could not, like many of her friends, break away from the church of Rome, and later she sacrificed her sympathies to her faith.

Michelangelo knew her about 1535, but their friendship did not really begin until the end of 1538. She was then forty-six years old and he was sixty-three.

It was a serious and devout friendship. They met on Sundays in the church of S. Silvestro at Monte Cavallo, and there they had those noble discussions which the Portuguese painter, Francis of Holland, has preserved for us in his four "Dialogues sur la Peinture," which took place in Rome in 1538–1539 and were written in 1548.

Then Vittoria, driven by her religious doubts, left Rome in 1541, to retire first to Orvieto to the cloister of S. Paolo and later to Viterbo to the cloister of S. Caterina near Cardinal Pole, her friend and spiritual guide. She returned to Rome from time to time to see Michelangelo and she wrote to him. We have only a very few of these letters which Michelangelo sacredly preserved. They are affectionate, but cold, and we feel that she was much more detached from him than he was from her. He often complains that she does not answer him. She wrote him:

"Magnificent Messer Michelangelo—I did not reply earlier to your letter because it was, as one might say, an answer to my last; for I thought that if you and I were to go on writing without intermission according to my obligation and your courtesy, I should have to neglect the Chapel of S. Catherine here, and be absent at the appointed hours for company with my sisterhood, while you would have to leave the Chapel of S. Paul, and be absent from morning through the day from your sweet usual colloquy with painted forms, the which with their natural accents do not speak to you less clearly than the living persons around me speak to me. Thus we should both of us fail in our duty, I to the brides, you to the vicar of Christ. For these reasons, inasmuch as I am well assured of our steadfast friendship and affection, bound by knots of Christian kindness, I do not think it necessary to obtain the proof of your good-will in letters by writing on my side, but rather to await with well-prepared mind some substantial occasion for serving you. Meanwhile I address my prayers to that Lord of whom you spoke to me with so fervent and humble a heart when I left Rome, that when I return thither I may find you with His image renewed and enlivened by true faith in your soul, in like measure as you have painted it with perfect art in my

Samaritan.[2] Believe me to remain always yours and your Urbino's."

In this way she merely made use of her powers to soothe her friend's spirit and to stimulate him to work. Most of all she relit that light of faith which had never ceased to burn in his soul, although enveloped in a night of doubt and despair. Besides "The Samaritan Woman at the Well," which is spoken of in the letter from Vittoria, Michelangelo made for her a drawing of a descent from the cross with these words of Dante, "Non vi si pensa, quaneo sangue costa," and a tragic crucifixion in which Jesus writhes as he implores Heaven. Perhaps the two admirable drawings of the Resurrection in the Louvre and the British Museum are of this same period.

Vittoria, in sending him, after 1539, her Sonetti Spirituali, also opened before his poetical genius another path to immortality.

Ever since his childhood he had made verses from an impelling need of expression. He covered his drawings, his letters and loose sheets of paper with thoughts in verse which he took up again and again, corrected and worked over ceaselessly. We have only a very few of these poems of his youth, for he burned many of them in 1518 with some drawings. He did not think them of value until he met the banker Luigi del Riccio and Donato Giannotti, who advised him to publish a collection of them. Donato took the matter up seriously about 1545. Michelangelo made a selection from his poems and his friends recopied them. But the death of Riccio in 1546 and perhaps also that of Vittoria in 1547 distracted him from this thought

[2] From the monastery at Viterbo, July 20, 1542 or 1543. The letter bears this address: "Al mio più che magnifico et più che carissimo M. Michel Agnolo Buanarroti." (Carteggio de Vittoria Colonna. Published by Ermanno Ferrero and Giuseppe Müller, Turin, 1892, pp. 268, 269.)

of worldly fame, and the poems remained unpublished until his death. Nevertheless they were passed from hand to hand and the most famous composers of the time, G. Archadelt, Bartolommeo Tromboncino, Costanzo Festa, Consilium—Italians, Frenchmen and Flemings—set his madrigals to music. Cultured people admired them, and Varchi, reading and commenting on one of these sonnets in 1546 before the Academy of Florence, declared that it had the clarity of the classic and the richness of the thought of Dante.

Michelangelo was in fact nourished on Dante. "No one understood him better or knew his works more perfectly," says Donato Giannotti, who placed him as arbiter in his dialogues on Dante in 1545.[3]

Michelangelo dedicated to Dante one of his most beautiful sonnets in which he envied his exile and his glory:

> Fuss'io pur lui! c'a tal fortuna nato,
> Per l'aspro esilio suo con la virtute
> Dare' del mundo il piu felice stato.[4]

He knew equally well all the other classics of Italian lyric poetry, Cavalcanti, Cino da Pistoia and Petrarch. His style is wrought from theirs, but his thought is entirely his own.

"You speak words only, but he speaks in deeds," wrote Francesco Berni to the poets of his time.

[3] Donato Giannotti, "De' gironi che Dante consumo nel cecrare l'Inferno e' Purgatorio. Dialoghi."

[4] Were I but he, born for like lingering pains
Against his exile coupled with his good,
I'd gladly change the world's best heritage.
(Translation of J. A. Symonds.)

Tacete umquanco pallide viole
Et liquidi cristalli et fere snelli:
Et dice cose, e voi dite parole.[5]

It is true that this was not achieved without a great obscurity of thought, remarked even by his contemporaries and which to us often makes their reading very difficult.

"He writes what Phœbus, Euterpe and the divine fury dictate to him, and afterward he hardly understands what he has written," says Lodovico Martelli.[6]

The sonnet form cramped him, and characteristically he loved that form because of its difficulty. He always delighted in doing violence to his genius and in making himself suffer. His poetry has often been compared to his sculpture. We can almost see him, as in Mariette's account,[7] making the chips of marble fly under his chisel or tearing from the block of his thought the idea that is haunting him, leaving it scarcely freed from the matrix. Frey, in his admirable edition, which is the only exact one of the "Rime" of Michelangelo, reveals the heroic fury with which he composed. He strikes only the main chord on his instrument, nothing more—no development, no variations. His dominant emotion once expressed, there is nothing more to say, the idea is exhausted. Most of his poems have remained in the condition of blocked-out torsos.

The most beautiful of these verses were written under the inspiration of Vittoria Colonna and the religious ideas

[5] Capitolo di Francesco Berni a fra Sebastiano del Piombo. (Rime. Ed. Frey, p. 263.)

[6] Canzone in lode di Michelagnolo Bonarroto. (See Frey, p. 7.)

[7] A Frenchman who saw him at that time.

which she revived in him. Separated from each other, they exchanged sonnets; she sent him forty from Viterbo[8] and he answered her in verse.[9]

In 1544 Vittoria returned to Rome to live in the cloister of S. Anna and remained there until her death on February 25, 1547. Her death prostrated Michelangelo. "He remained for a long time stupefied and out of his senses," says Condivi. But the faith which she had given back to him never again left him. The death of his friend only deepened it, and the two strange and powerful sonnets which celebrate that death[10] are a hymn of triumphant faith and love.

When Michelangelo finally left Florence in 1534 and went to settle in Rome he expected to be at last free and able to discharge his debt to the memory of Julius II. But no sooner was the new pope elected than he hastened to attach Michelangelo to himself. He was Paulo III Farnese, "a choleric man, ambitious, daring, full of intelligence and cunning, ostentatious, one of the last great popes of the Renaissance and the one who perhaps did the most to beautify Rome, the great builder among the popes of the sixteenth century."[11]

He summoned Michelangelo, overwhelmed him with promises, and asked him to work for him.

Michelangelo wanted to decline, alleging as excuse his old contracts with the heirs of Julius II, but Paul III was

[8] Letters of Michelangelo to Fattucci, March 7, 1551.
[9] Rime. Ed. Frey, LXXXVIII, p. 93.
[10] *Ibid.*, C and CL, pp. 105, 106.
[11] The work on the fortifications of Rome directed by Antonio da San Gallo dates from his reign and also the construction of the Capitol, the raising of the statue of Marcus Aurelius, the completion of the Farnese Palace, the construction of the Via Paola, of the Sala Regia and the Pauline Chapel at the Vatican, the Caffarelli and Spada palaces, the Villa Medici, etc.

furious and declared that he would tear up all those contracts and that Michelangelo should work for him in spite of everything. Michelangelo thought of taking flight to Urbino or to Genoa to his friend, the bishop of Almeria, but he gave in as usual, too weak to resist. The pope, who came with ten of his cardinals to see the statues already completed for the monument of Julius II, went into ecstasies over them, especially over the Moses, of which the Cardinal of Mantua said that "that figure alone would be enough to honour the memory of Pope Julius," and he was even more determined than before to reserve Michelangelo exclusively for his own plans.

On September 1, 1535, he appointed him by official letters architect-in-chief, sculptor and painter to the Apostolic Palace with a salary for life of twelve hundred golden crowns a year, of which six hundred were the revenue (uncertain and at once contested) of a toll-bridge on the Po near Placentia.[12]

Ever since April, 1535, Michelangelo had agreed to work on the Last Judgment. The idea of completing the decoration of the Sistine Chapel with that fresco originated with Clement VII, who had already talked to Michelangelo about it in 1533. At that time the plan also included a Fall of Lucifer[13] on the entrance wall of the Sistine.

The first thing to be done was to destroy the frescoes of Perugino which covered the great wall below the altar.[14]

[12] As a matter of fact, Michelangelo did not actually receive any income from this source until 1538, and after many difficulties he lost it in 1547.

[13] Later on the subject was treated after the sketches of Michelangelo in the Chapel of S. Gregorio at Santa Trinità. (See Vasari.)

[14] Perugino had painted the Assumption with a portrait of Sextius IV kneeling, Moses saved from the waters, and the Birth of Christ.

This did not, of course, trouble Michelangelo, who despised Perugino and called him a "blockhead." He worked on the Last Judgment from 1536 to 1541.[15]

While he was working at it probably in 1539 he fell from the scaffold and injured himself seriously in the leg. Still he completed his immense task by December 25, 1541, the day when the public was admitted to see it.

No one of his works has been more diversely judged. Before considering it at all, we should remember that it was the work of an old man between sixty and sixty-six. The vitality which this "terrible" man still possessed after a life of exhausting labours and troubles is, whatever we may think of the work, something superhuman. The first thing which strikes us in that colossal fresco twenty metres high and ten wide and swarming with hundreds of figures, is order, reason and imperious will, controlled and almost cold. The innumerable human bodies, a throng which produces at first a sense of stifling discomfort, are gathered in a dozen groups which balance each other and are all drawn along in a dizzying whirl from right to left around the Christ.

If we turn to the drama itself we are overwhelmed by an impression of brutal force. Force alone rules. There is no soul; nothing but unreasoning physical force and the terror of it. The moment chosen is terrible. Through the thunder of the trumpets blown to bursting by the angels, the herculean Christ curses.

"Now there is no longer any time for pity or room for pardon."[16]

[15] Léon Dorez has found recently in the records of the private accounts of Paul III the exact dates of the work, April–May, 1536, to November 18, 1541.

[16] Thus Vittoria Colonna had herself described the Last Judgment to Michelangelo: "Christ comes twice, the first time he is all gentleness; he only shows his great kindness, his clemency and his

Before that implacable gesture which launches eternal death all the army of gigantic bodies swerves and bows, a prey to one feeling—that of fear; crushing, horrible fear relieved by no reasoning thought, a fear of blows like that of a dog under the whip. The tremendous vigour of these trembling athletes throws more harshly into relief their abject helplessness. The martyrs in order to recall to the Master their claims on His mercy exhibit servilely the instruments of their martyrdom. St. Laurence covers himself with his gridiron; St. Blaise waves his rack; St. Bartholomew holds out his bloody skin and lifts his bare knife with such ferocity that he appears rather to be the flayer than the flayed. The Virgin withdraws into the background so as not to see. Abel hides behind Adam, and one of his sisters throws herself, terrified, on Eve's knees and buries her face in the arms of her mother. The tempest howls above. The heavy flight of angels rolls through space, head over heels, bearing with an exaggerated and forced violence the column, the cross and the instruments of the Passion. Below at the right is a savage mêlée of souls and angels in a hand-to-hand struggle. At the left the bodies rise heavily from Purgatory like inflated balloons drawn up by the sun. At the bottom is the monstrous harvest of the earth giving up its dead; Hell, full of the atrocious horror of suffering and the still more atrocious joy of creating suffering. "Charon with eyes like burning coals, who smites with his oars." The maddened

---

pity; he comes for the sinners and the sick, to give peace, light and forgiveness, all glowing with charity, clothed in humanity. . . . The second time he comes armed and shows his justice, his majesty, his grandeur and his almighty power, and there is no longer any time for pity or room for pardon. (Letter of Vittoria between 1535–1546, probably to Bernadino Ochino,—Carteggio de Vittoria Colonna, p. 242.)

damned, crowded together like a herd of sheep, demons grabbing shrieking souls who hide their eyes and ears with horror, the falling of bodies which come down like masses of lead, and in the extreme right-hand corner Minos, evil and undisturbed.

There is in such a work a mass of wrath, vengeance and hate which is suffocating. If it was not purified by colossal and almost elementary force it would be insupportable.

This, then, is what the Prophets and the Sibyls are looking forward to, this is what the convulsive agony of the paintings of the ceiling predicts. This implacable conclusion of human history conformed perfectly to the essence of Christian thought, but the expression of it was so audacious and so stripped of all compromise that it revolted the majority of Christians, whom Michelangelo, aristocratic in his faith as in his whole spirit, never considered at all.

It was not only Biagio da Cesina,[17] Master of Ceremonies to Paul III, who declared the painting to be "improper".—"opera da stufe o d'osterie" (work fit only for a bagnio or an inn), but the majority of Catholic opinion agreed. Aretino sounded the alarm. He might not seem to be very well qualified to do this, but he wanted to revenge himself on Michelangelo, who had not shown that regard for him which the Master Singer knew how to exact even from kings.[18] The author of "The Hypocrite,"[19] the prototype of Tartuffe, was also the model.

"Messire," he wrote in November, 1545, "as a baptised

[17] We know that Michelangelo, to revenge himself, portrayed Biagio from memory in the Hell of his Last Judgment under the form of Minos with a huge serpent wound about his legs in the midst of a mountain of devils. (Vasari.)

[18] We must not, however, imagine that Michelangelo any more

man I am ashamed of the license which you have permitted yourself in expressing your conception of that end toward which turn all the aspirations of our true faith. Now behold that this Michelangelo, a man of such astounding fame and universally admired, has exposed to the world as much impiety and irreligion as perfection of painting. Is it possible that you, who, being divine, do not condescend to have commerce with men, is it possible that you have done this in the greatest temple of God, above the highest altar of Christ, in the most sacred chapel in the world, where the great hinges of the church, the venerable pontiffs, the Vicars of Christ, by the Catholic ceremonies and holy prayers confess, contemplate and adore His body and blood? In so lofty a representation you draw saints and angels, the first without any terrestrial decency and the others deprived of all celestial honours. Remember the Pagans, who, when they made statues of Diana, clothed her and even made the naked Venus cover with her hands those parts which should not be shown, and behold here a Christian, who, placing art above faith, holds it a royal spectacle not to observe equal decency toward the martyrs and the virgins, and shows gestures so coarse that even women of the street would

---

than his contemporaries had the courage to show openly to Aretino the contempt which he must have felt for him. If he declined the offer of collaboration in the Last Judgment which Aretino had baldly made him and for which he had outlined a detailed program, it was only with many compliments and much flattery. (Letter of September, 1537.) Even though Aretino did not obtain from him the gift for which he asked, we find, nevertheless, that he had received in September, 1535, through Vasari, a head in wax and a sketch for a St. Catherine. But he did not consider himself satisfied.

[19] The "Hypocrite," dedicated to Guidobaldo II, Duke of Urbino. (See Pierre Gaultier, "L'Aretin," 1895.)

shut their eyes so as not to see them. Such a style belongs only in a voluptuous bagnio and not in the most holy chapel. It would be a lesser crime not to believe than to attack in such a way the faith of others. Already the excellence of these indiscreet wonders has been punished, since they have accomplished the miracle of killing your glory. Therefore regain your honour by placing flames of fire over the shameful parts of the damned, and rays of sunlight over those of the saved, or, still better, imitate the modesty of the Florentines, who hid under golden leaves the belly of your beautiful colossal David, even though that stood in a public square and not in a sacred place. May God forgive you. I do not say this to you through resentment at not having received what I asked you for, although you should have sent me what you agreed, and you would have done well to have taken the greatest possible trouble about it, for you would in that way put an end to the rumours which say that no one can get anything from you but Gherardi and Tomai.[20] But if the treasure which Julius II left you so that his remains should be placed in a monument carved by you, has not been enough to make you keep your promises, what could I expect? Anyway, it is a fact that your failure to redeem that debt is considered as a theft. . . . But since our souls have more need of faith than of lifelikeness of drawing, may God inspire his Holiness, Paul III, as He inspired the blessed Gregory who decided to strip Rome of the superb statues of the idols rather than to do harm through them to the respect due to the humble images of the saints! Finally, to sum up, if you had taken counsel in your com-

---

[20] Gherardo Perini and Tommaso dei Cavalieri—thus Aretino in passing adds to the accusation of impiety an allusion to the evil reports about the habits of Michelangelo. Two lines lower down he will accuse him of theft.

position of the universe, the abyss and paradise of the glorious and terrible sketch which I sent you and of my instructions, and of the knowledge which the world has so praised in me, I dare say that no one would have regretted it."[21]

This venomous letter was, unluckily, not a simple act of vengeance and of blackmail. It was the hypocritical echo of many sincere protestations. A Florentine in 1549 called Michelangelo "the creator of that vileness, irreproachable in art but not in faith," and he added, "All the modern painters and sculptors imitate such Lutheran abominations.[22] They paint and carve even in the least important churches only such figures as are calculated to destroy faith and devotion; but I hope that some day God will send His saints to overthrow such idolatries." The trial of Veronese in a certain measure justifies these accusations. Brought before the Inquisition on July 18, 1573, for the indecency of his Feast in the House of Simon, Veronese did not fail to intrench himself behind the example of the Last Judgment.[23] It is true that the Inquisition undertook nobly the defense of Michelangelo against him.

"Do you not know that in representing the Last Judgment, in which we can not imagine any clothing, there was no ground for painting any? But what is there in those figures that is not inspired by the Holy Spirit? There are neither buffoons nor dogs, nor arms or other mockeries. . . ."

---

[21] *In postscript:* Now that I have a little discharged my anger against the cruelty with which you have repaid my devotion, and have made you see, I believe, that if you are "divino" I am not "d'acqua," tear up this letter as I do, and reflect. For I am a man to whom even Kings and Emperors answer.

[22] Gaye Carteggio, Vol. II, p. 500.

[23] A Baschet "P. Veronese devant le Saint Office," 1880.

But Rome had not so lofty a spirit; the ideas of Biagio and Aretino made their way. Neither the European glory of Michelangelo nor his favour with the popes nor the respect inspired by the nobility of his life and his well-known faith succeeded in protecting the Last Judgment from the zeal of the bigots. Paul IV Caraffa had for a while the idea of covering up the entire fresco. By his order Daniele da Volterra clothed the nakedness which wounded Aretino's modesty (in 1559–1560) and gained for this the surname of "Braghettone."

Under Pius V in 1566 Girolamo da Fano continued this holy work. This was not enough to satisfy the wrath of the good people, for in 1596 Clement VIII Aldobrandini again wanted to have the Judgment painted out. He was prevented by a protest from the Academy of St. Luke.[24] Indeed, until the eighteenth century the work of Michelangelo was shamelessly redressed, retouched and repainted.[25] It is therefore impossible to judge today exactly of the original appearance and especially of the colour, the harmony of which has been outrageously destroyed.[26] Michelangelo, unmoved, watched the mutilation of his work. He was asked his opinion, and he answered with-

[24] "Missirini: Memorie per servire alla storia della romana Accademia di S. Luca." (Cited by E. Muntz, "Histoire de l'Art pendant la Renaissance," Vol. III, p. 126.)

[25] In 1762 Stefano Pozzi was polishing it under Clement VIII. Abbé Richard, in his "Voyage d'Italie," says that he saw "some very mediocre artists occupied in covering with draperies the most beautiful nude figures of the painting and of the ceiling."

[26] The only document which makes it possible for us to give an account of the original work is a copy by Marcello Venusti in the Museum of Naples, from which a painter of Orléans, Robert Le Noyer, seems to have made in 1750 a reduced copy which is now in the Museum of Montpellier. (See G. Lafenestre et E. Richtenberger, "La Peinture en Europe." Rome.)

out anger and with calm contempt: "Say to his Holiness that this is a little thing which can easily be put in order. Let him attend to putting the world in order; to reform a painting is not much trouble."

In spite of everything the Last Judgment was the school of the world. Men came from all over Italy and from abroad to be present at its unveiling on December 25, 1541. Hosts of Italian, French, Flemish and German artists followed each other without respite through the Sistine Chapel, copying zealously the entire fresco, and the glory of Michelangelo, far from being diminished as Aretino predicted, became colossal on account of it.

"That sublime painting," writes Vasari, "should serve as a model in our art. Divine Providence made this present to the world to show how much intelligence she could bestow on certain men whom she sends to the earth. The most learned draughtsman will tremble when he sees those bold outlines and those marvellous foreshortenings. In the presence of that celestial work our senses are paralysed and we ask ourselves what will exist of the works which were made before this and the works that will be made after it. One can call oneself happy when one has seen this prodigy of art and of genius. O fortunate Paul III! Heaven has allowed you to be the patron of that glory. Your name will live forever beside that of Buonarroti whose fame fills the universe."

The fresco of the Sistine was hardly finished when the insatiable Paul III insisted that Michelangelo, in spite of his extreme old age, should paint the frescoes of the Pauline Chapel. With a great effort he completed the conversion of St. Paul and the Crucifixion of St. Peter which, begun in 1542, injured after 1545 by a fire, interrupted by two severe illnesses in 1544 and 1546, were finally completed in 1549–1550. "He complained," says Vasari, "that he had suffered greatly in executing these works. Painting, and especially fresco, is not fitted for an old man." He was, as a matter of fact, seventy-five years old. Both frescoes to-day have almost disappeared. In spite of the exaggeration of the attitudes and the abuse of virtuosity Michelangelo had preserved in them his rough vigour, and we can still see there a tumultuous force which struggles in darkness.[27]

During this fifteen years' work the old man had lost all hope of ever finishing the monument of Julius II, and had with great difficulty prevented Paul III from taking some of the statues to serve as ornaments of the Pauline Chapel. He had had to sign, on August 20, 1542, a fifth and last contract with the heirs of Julius II. By this agreement he relinquished for the time being three statues, which must have been the Moses and the two Slaves.[28] Then he decided that the Slaves were not any longer fitted to the tomb and he began two other figures, Active Life and Contemplative Life.[29]

In addition, Michelangelo agreed to give fourteen hundred crowns[30] to his pupil Urbino and to Raffaelli da

[27] The British Museum and the University of Oxford have drawings which are related to these frescoes. The Cartoon is in the Museum at Naples.

[28] March 6, 1542. (Gaye, Vol. II, p. 289.)

[29] July 20, 1542 (Petition of Michelangelo to Paul III), Michelangelo added that the two figures were already so far advanced that they could be easily completed by other artists. (Gaye, Vol. II, p. 297.)

[30] The fourteen hundred crowns had been deposited at the bank of Silvestro da Montanto & Co. They were to be divided as follows: eight hundred for the work of Urbino; five hundred and thirty for the statues of Raffaelli da Montelupo, whose Madonna was already finished; and fifty for the transportation and placing of the statues by Urbino.

Montelupo for finishing the monument, after which he was to be free from all obligation forever.

But he had not reached the end of his troubles, for the heirs of Julius II continued persecuting the poor man with insulting demands for money which they pretended to have previously disbursed to him. Michelangelo went almost mad, as he had done in the time of Clement VII over the Medici Chapel, and it was in vain that Paul III commanded him not to think about it, but to give himself up entirely to his painting of the Pauline Chapel.

He answered, "You paint with your head and not with your hands. Who does not think for himself dishonours himself. That is why I can do nothing good so long as I have these preoccupations. I have been chained to this trouble all my life," he continued, bitterly, "I have lost my youth over it; I have been ruined by my too great conscientiousness. It is my fate; I see many people who live tranquilly on an income of two or three thousand crowns and I have only succeeded after a terrible struggle in being poor."[31]

To satisfy his creditors he finished with his own hands the statues of Active Life and Contemplative Life,[32] although he was not obliged to do so.

At last the monument of Julius II was finished and shown in the Church of S. Pietro in Vincoli in February, 1545. What was left of the beautiful original plan? Only the Moses which had become the central figure after having been merely one of the details. Would the complete work have been a prodigy analogous for sculpture to what

[31] October, 1542. Letter to an unknown person whom he calls Monsignore.
[32] 18 November, 1542. Letter of Michelangelo to Luigi del Riccio.

the Sistine Chapel is for painting? Certainly no prophet of the Sistine Chapel attains to the sovereign perfection of the Moses.

The Moses is a supernatural and savage apparition half beast, half god. Pagan? Christian? No one knows. Two horns pierce the narrow skull, a flowing beard descends from his face to his knees like a parasitical vine attached to a great tree. He seems calm, but in his terrible jaw with close-shut teeth and projecting lower lip is wrath which shatters and crushes like the first chords of the overture to "Coriolanus." An implacable and murderous force, a tumult of rage and contempt wars in the silence of that arrogant being, with his huge bulk, his knotted arms—less brutal than those of most of Michelangelo's heroes, and with strong and beautiful hands—and left leg bent ready to rise. The dress is a barbarous one. No other work of Michelangelo is as completely finished. We feel that he had lived with it more than thirty years without being willing to let it go. He could see himself in it as in a superb mirror which gave him back the image that he had divined of his own soul. For the Moses is not only the most perfect artistic expression of his genius, but also its highest moral expression. Nowhere else has he so completely realised the majestic balance of a violent and passionate soul controlled by an iron will. Everywhere else passion is let loose and the human being is given into its hands. Here the savage elements are in suspense, ready to fuse. It is a thunder-cloud charged with lightning.

Beside that superhuman creation rich with the whole life of Michelangelo, the two gracious figures of Leah and Rachel the work of his old age, seem a little cold and affected.

"I seemed in a dream to see a lady, young and beautiful, going through a meadow, gathering flowers, and singing she was saying, 'Let him know, whoso asks my name, that I am Leah, and I go moving my fair hands around to make myself a garland. To please me at the glass here I adorn me, but my sister Rachel never withdraws from her mirror, and sits all day. She is as fain to look with her fair eyes as I to adorn me with my hands. Her seeing, and me doing, satisfies.' "[33]

The perfume of these lovely verses of Dante penetrates Michelangelo's two statues, which are rather apart from the rest of his work. If it were not for the largeness of their conception they would recall by their "morbidezza" and their cold grace the style of Civitale and Rossellino. Michelangelo seems here to be softened and a little tamed.

The symbolical meaning of these figures is obscure, as usual with him. His intellectual quality was rarely strong enough or rather clear enough to impose itself on his artistic conceptions. It is placed in juxtaposition to them in a puerile and accessory way as in the allegorical attributes of the Medici tombs, and we can take it away without hurting the strength of the work.

[33] Giovane e bella in sogno mi parea
  Donna vedere andar per una landa
  Cogliendo fiori; e cantando dicea:

  Sappia, qualunque il mio nome domanda
  Ch'io mi son Lia, e vo movendo intorno
  La belle mani a farmi una ghirlanda.

  Per piacermi allo specchio qui m'adorno;
  Ma mia suora Rachel mai non si smaga
  Dal suo miraglio, e siede tutto giorno

  Ell' è de' suoi begli occhi veder vaga,
  Com' io dell' adornami con la mani;
  Lei lo vedere, e mi l'oprare appaga.
                              —(Purgatorio, XXVII.)
                    (Translation of C. E. Norton.)

As for the rest of the monument of Julius II, it is not worth mentioning.[34] It is a caricature of the great project, but at least it was finished. Michelangelo was delivered from the nightmare of his whole life.

[34] A Prophet and a Sibyl are by Raffaelli da Montelupo, and the absurd statue of the Pope by Maso Boscoli da Fiesole.

Chapter 5

Old Age and Death (1547–1564)

MICHELANGELO CARED no longer for his own glory. He thought only of the glory of God, and art had become to him merely a means of service. He wrote, "I understand now how great is the mistake, the passionate delusion in which I made of art an idol and a king."

> L'affectuosa fantasia,
> Che l'arte mi fece idol'e monarca,
> Conosco or ben, com' era d'error carca. . . .[1]

His soul "had turned to that divine love which welcomes us with arms outspread upon the cross."

[1] Now know I well that fond phantasy
   Which made my soul the worshipper and thrall
   Of Earthly Art, is vain.

(Translation of J. A. Symonds.)

L'anima, volta a quell' amor divino
C'aperse a prender noi' n croce le braccia.

He wished to consecrate all that remained of his life to the task of building for his God the temple of temples, St. Peter's.

By a pontifical letter of Paul III, dated January 1, 1547, and renewed by Julius III in 1552 he had been appointed governor and architect of St. Peter's with full power to carry on the construction. He accepted this heavy task as a sacred duty, and refused to take any pay for it. In 1557 he wrote to his nephew Lionardo, "many people believe, as I do myself, that I have been placed at this post by God. I will not leave it because I am serving for the love of God and put all my hope in Him."[2]

He at once found himself in trouble with the party of San Gallo. They had always been his enemies and it must be acknowledged that he had done his best to deserve their hostility.

When Raphael was directing the work on St. Peter's, Antonio da San Gallo had been his assistant, and he therefore belonged to the party opposed to Michelangelo. In 1537 San Gallo became architect-in-chief, succeeding Baldassare Peruzzi, and he abandoned, as Raphael had done, Bramante's great design for the main construction. Michelangelo, on the contrary, went back to that plan, for whatever rancour he might feel against Bramante personally, his genius bowed before that of the great architect. He wrote in 1555 to Bartolommeo Ammanati, "It can not be denied that in architecture Bramante was greater than any other man since classic times. He conceived the first design for St. Peter's, simple, clear and

_____

[2] July, 1557. Letter of Michelangelo to Lionardo Buonarroti.

free from all confusion, and whoever like San Gallo has turned aside from this plan has turned aside from the truth."

Before the disagreement over St. Peter's, Michelangelo had twice come into sharp conflict with San Gallo over the fortifications of the Borgo and the completion of the Farnese palace.

Paul III wished to reconstruct and complete the fortifications of Rome which had been destroyed in 1527. San Gallo had been engaged on them since 1534, but the work had only been actively pushed since 1542. In February, 1545, meetings were held under the presidency of Pier Luigi Farnese in the Castle of St. Angelo to discuss the subject of the fortifications of the Borgo, and to these Michelangelo was summoned. He expressed opinions absolutely opposed to those of San Gallo and enumerated the faults already committed in the works. Hot words were exchanged, and the pope was obliged to command both men to be silent. Soon after this affair Michelangelo made a new design for the fortifications, involving the destruction of San Gallo's work, and this was accepted.[8]

Michelangelo added to this defeat another more bitter still. San Gallo had built the Farnese palace up to the second story, but his plans for the third story and the cornice did not please the pope, who turned them over to Michelangelo to be mercilessly criticised. A competition was opened in 1546 for the cornice in which Perino del Vaga, Sebastiano del Piombo, Vasari and Michelangelo

[8] See Vasari. In October, 1546, Michelangelo with Jacopo Meleghino was commissioned to direct the fortification of the Borgo. He was undoubtedly subordinate to the orders of Pier Luigi Farnese, who was replaced after his death in 1547 by Jacopo Fusto Castriotto d'Urbino. Toward the end of 1547 they were at work on the bastion of the Belvedere. (See Gotti.)

took part. Michelangelo's design was accepted, and when San Gallo died from this humiliation in October, 1546, the direction of the work on the palace passed at once into his hands. Michelangelo set aside the original plan entirely and built the third story on the court on the Corinthian order. He also built the beautiful cornice, so broad and fine in conception, in which he had possibly the assistance of Vignole or Guglielmo della Porta. Even San Gallo's death did not disarm Michelangelo, who searched relentlessly for the malpractices committed under his predecessor in the work on St. Peter's and who raged against the guilty with a violence which Vasari still echoes when he says, "Michelangelo delivered St. Peter's from thieves and bandits."

It is easy to imagine what hatred these proceedings awakened in San Gallo's party, supported by all the contractors and foremen whose faults Michelangelo had denounced and prosecuted. The members of the committee of administration themselves were accomplices.[4]

A coalition was formed against him which had for its chief Nanni di Baccio Bigio, the rascally architect whom Vasari accuses of having stolen Michelangelo's plans even before this trouble. From the very beginning of Michelangelo's direction at St. Peter's Nanni spread the rumour that he knew nothing of architecture, that his model was

[4] Michelangelo wrote to the committee: "You know that I told Balduccio not to send his lime unless it was good. He has sent bad lime and won't admit that he can be forced to take it back, which proves that he has an understanding with the person who accepted it. Such things encourage the effrontery of those whom I have dismissed for similar frauds. Whoever accepts bad materials or bribes corrupts justice. I beg of you, in the name of the authority which I have received from the pope, never more to accept anything which can not be used, even if it came from Heaven. I do not want anyone to believe that I shut my eyes to these irregularities."

childish, that he squandered the money and hid himself to work at night for fear that his blunders would be seen. It was also rumoured that the cornice of the Farnese palace was in danger of falling. Michelangelo was exasperated. "Who are these rogues, these triple scoundrels," he wrote to the committee of administration, "who, after they had spread lies about my work on the Farnese palace, lied still more in the report that they sent to the committee of St. Peter's?"

The committee, instead of defending him, joined in the chorus of his calumniators. They sent a protest to the pope because, they said, he kept them entirely ignorant of his plans, which he showed to no one, while he destroyed the work of his predecessor. They wished to be freed from any responsibility for such proceedings, especially for "the destruction which had been and continued to be so great that all who witnessed it were greatly disturbed."

They succeeded in bringing about in 1551 a meeting at St. Peter's under the presidency of the pope, where all the builders and foremen, supported by the Cardinals Salviati and Marcello Cervini (the future pope, Marcellus II), testified against Michelangelo. Vasari describes the scene for us. At this time Michelangelo had already finished the main apse with the three chapels and the three windows above them, but no one knew yet how he would vault the church, and all agreed in prophesying that the lighting would be insufficient. Michelangelo, when he was questioned by Cardinal Cervini, explained that besides the three windows already built there would be three more in the vault, which was to be built of travertine. "You never told us anything about that," said the cardinal. "I am not obliged to tell your lordships or anyone else what I intend to do," replied Michelangelo; "your business is to take

charge of the expenses and to see that no one steals. The
building is my affair." He then turned to the pope and
said, "Holy Father, you see what my pay is. If the mis-
eries I endure do not help my soul it is all time and trouble lost."

The pope, who loved him, placed his hands on his
shoulders and said: "You gain for both your soul and
your body. Have no fear."[5]

Without the favour of the pope he could not have held
out for a moment against the enmity which his haughty
and contemptuous ways roused against him. Therefore
when Paul III died and Marcellus II succeeded him (April
9, 1555) Michelangelo was on the point of leaving Rome,
but by the twenty-third of May Marcellus had died and
Paul IV took his place. Michelangelo, again sure of the
highest protection, went on with his fight. He would have
thought himself dishonoured and would have feared for
his salvation if he had given up the work. "Against my
will," he wrote in 1555, "I was entrusted with this task,
and for eight years I have exhausted myself in vain in the
midst of all kinds of trouble and weariness. Now that the
construction is so far advanced that I can begin to vault
the dome, to leave Rome would be to ruin the whole
work, a great shame to me and for my soul a great sin."[6]

In 1557 Cosmo de' Medici begged him to come back
to Florence "where honour and rest awaited him," but he
answered firmly, "I can not leave here until I have carried the construction of St. Peter's so far that my plan
can not be changed or destroyed and there will no longer
be any possibility for thieves to begin their work again, as
these scoundrels are only waiting for a chance to do. This
is my resolve."

[5] Vasari.
[6] Letter of Michelangelo to his nephew Lionardo, May 11, 1555.

That same year his friends, who were afraid that he would carry his great designs with him into the grave, for none of them were written down, urged and besought until they succeeded in persuading him to execute a model in wood of the dome of St. Peter's.[7] He was still working on this in 1560.

The building went on, but not without many difficulties. It was necessary in 1557 to rebuild almost the entire vault of the Chapel of the King of France because Michelangelo had been ill and unable to watch the work closely enough.

The attacks on him began again with fresh vigour at each mistake, and some of his friends, like Cardinal Carpi, joined in them. Michelangelo heard from Francesco Bandini that the cardinal said everywhere that the work on St. Peter's could not be worse managed. Much hurt, he wrote to him at once that, "although he felt sure that the work was going on well, he feared that possibly his own enthusiasm and his age had blinded him and were, without his knowing it, a source of harm and danger to the building." In consequence he begged that they "would be so kind as to relieve him of the load which he had carried without pay for seventeen years under the orders of the popes." He offered his resignation. "A greater favour than its acceptance," he said, "could not be accorded him."[8]

His resignation was not accepted, and Pius IV in a pontifical letter gave him full powers and forbade that his plans should be set aside.

But Nanni di Baccio Bigio, indefatigable in his hate, moved heaven and earth to drive him away. In 1562

[7] Particularly Cardinal Carpi, Tommaso dei Cavalieri, Donato Giannotti, Francesco Bandini and Gio. Francesco Lottini.
[8] Letter of September 13, 1560.

Nanni appealed to Cosmo de' Medici for his aid in securing the appointment of architect of St. Peter's. Cosmo answered that he would do nothing about it while Michelangelo lived.

In 1563 the struggle became a tragic one. The head of the work at St. Peter's, Cesare de Casteldurante, was stabbed, and Pier Luigi Gaeta, Michelangelo's friend and one of his best aids, was thrown into prison on a false accusation of theft. Michelangelo responded to this by appointing Gaeta in Cesare's place. The committee of administration dismissed Gaeta and put Nanni in his place, and Michelangelo, beside himself with rage, no longer went to St. Peter's. His enemies did not lose this chance to spread the report that he was no longer willing to take charge of the building, and Michelangelo denied this in vain. The committee nominated a successor, and this successor was of course Nanni. Nanni cut loose at once from his master and began to give orders, for he thought that the old man of eighty-eight, weary at last of the struggle, would be forced either to submit or to resign. He did not know his antagonist. Michelangelo went at once to the pope and told him that if justice was not done he would leave Rome and go to Florence. The pope called the committee together and the members accused Michelangelo of having committed errors which endangered the whole building. Michelangelo asked for an investigation and summoned Nanni to show the mistakes of which he accused him. Nanni could show nothing but his own bad faith, and was dismissed in disgrace.[9]

[9] Vasari. See in the excellent work of Henry Thode, "Michelangelo und das Ende der Renaissance," Vol. I, the detailed account of these struggles of Michelangelo with the faction of San Gallo and Nanni di Baccio Bigio.

This did not prevent Nanni from sending, five months later just after the death of Michelangelo, a letter by the Florentine ambassador to Cosmo de' Medici, asking again to be appointed his successor.

Until his last hour Michelangelo met with this fierce opposition over the work on St. Peter's, but his faith and his fighting spirit found in this only another reason for persevering.

While Michelangelo had taken Bramante's design for the church and rested on his authority, he had in the course of construction introduced many important modifications into the plan, and stamped the whole monument with the imprint of his own grandiose and heavy genius.

He kept the Greek cross with equal arms and four apses, at the same time hiding the apse of the façade in a rectangular mass against which he wished to put a portico with four gigantic columns. He suppressed the salient angles and the towers which should have risen at the extremities of the four arms of the cross. The beautiful clean-cut lines of the curved ends of these arms, which in Bramante's plan stretched out in the form of a semicircular tribune, were smothered in a massive, vigorous envelope which gave the construction the effect of a fortified bastion.

The most beautiful part of the work was the famous dome, where the influence of Brunelleschi combined with the conception of Bramante. Michelangelo said once while he was working on S. Lorenzo in Florence that "it was possible to do differently from Brunelleschi, but not to do better."

He did not fail to remember the masterly dome of S. Maria de Fiore, for as soon as he was appointed to St. Peter's he had the exact measures of this dome from the lantern to the ground, and also the height sent to him.

The dimensions that he chose for St. Peter's seem to have been inspired by them.[10]

Bramante in his design as shown by Burckhardt and de Geymueller[11] gave the principal importance to a circular colonnade crowned by statues on which the dome seemed to rest. Michelangelo concentrated his attention on the dome itself, subordinating, as ever, grace and harmony to majesty and force. He accentuated the buttresses of the drum with pairs of columns and raised the outer dome of the cupola, whose beautiful curve possesses an impetuous quality which recalls, with less passion and more freedom, the huge octagonal dome of Brunelleschi, crouching on its base like a beast ready to spring.[12] The lofty serenity of the dome of St. Peter's is almost unique in the work of Michelangelo. He had lived so long with the thoughts of Raphael and Bramante that at last their smile was reflected in his work.[13]

Besides this great masterpiece other architectural works filled the end of his life—the rebuilding of the Capitol, the Porta Pia, S. Maria degli Angeli and S. Giovanni dei Fiorentini.

[10] See Anatole de Montaiglon, "La Vie de Michel-Ange." ("L'-Œuvre et la Vie de Michel-Ange," p. 288.)

[11] H. de Geymueller, "Ursprüngliche Entwürfe zu S. Peter."

[12] The cupola of St. Peter's, like that of Florence, has two concentric domes. It was to have had three according to Michelangelo's model, but Guglielmo della Porta, who carried out the plans after his death, left out the lower one.

[13] Michelangelo had also the rather unfortunate idea of flanking the main cupola by four little domes (of which only two were made) instead of the four towers which were to frame it in Bramante's plan. Michelangelo did not have the happiness of seeing his work completed for at his death the cupola was only finished as far as the drum. Guglielmo della Porta finished the dome in a year.

It was in 1548 that Michelangelo presided over the erection of the statue of Marcus Aurelius in the square before the Capitol, but his first sketch for the palaces were no earlier than 1546, and when he died the buildings were far from finished.

He never saw the stairway or the colonnades. An engraving of Pérac's executed in 1559 after Michelangelo's own drawings, "ex ipso exemplari Michaelis Bonaroti," and reproduced in the *Speculum Romanie Magnificentiæ* of Lafreri, show exactly what his plan was and take from him all blame for the incoherencies and vulgarities put into the execution after his death. The beautiful double staircase of the Senatorial Palace and the fountain with the river gods is all his own; but he had meant to put a colonnade crowned by pilasters at the top of the stairway, the windows of the upper story should have been higher and the campanile crenellated.[14] The Porta Pia was at the end of a long street which ran from the Monte Cavallo.[15]

[14] See "Michaelis, Zeitschrift für bildende kunst." 1891, Vol. III, p. 184 *et seq.*; E. Müntz, "Histoire de l'art pendant le Renaissance," Vol. III, pp. 338–340. The palace of the Senate was built in 1546 to 1568, the two staircases in 1555. The façade of the Palazzo dei Conservatori dates from after the death of Michelangelo; the campanile is the work of Martino Lunghi, and dates from 1579. The groups of the Dioscuri were installed in 1583. From 1592 to 1598 the façade of the palace of the Senate was rebuilt and changed. The Capitoline Museum dates from the seventeenth century under the pontificate of Innocent X.

We must be very careful not to blame Michelangelo for the faults of his successors as Charles Garnier has done in a too severe article published in "L'Œuvre et la de Michel-Ange," in which he nevertheless acknowledges that he was thinking of the Capitol when he built the Loggia of the Opera House at Paris. He adds it is true that he had "studied the proportions with great care and skill, and I can say without blushing, with more talent."

[15] Michelangelo also made drawings for the other gates of Rome. (Vasari.)

Michelangelo made three designs for it in 1561, of which Pius IV chose the most reasonable, according to Vasari. This was more to the credit of the pope than the artist, for the plan which was carried out shows, with a few remnants of massive and imperious power, a complete lack of good taste.

He also worked in 1560–1561 at the transformation of the great hall in the baths of Diocletian into the church of S. Maria degli Angeli, but it is almost impossible to judge this now, for his work was entirely changed and disfigured in 1746 by Vanvitelli.

He was no more fortunate with the Church of S. Giovanni dei Fiorentini at Rome, which was another of his great projects, undertaken with enthusiasm and ending in nothing. S. Giovanni had been begun under Leo X by Jacopo Sansovino. Antonio da San Gallo had worked on it later and had made a model of the church, and then the construction had been abandoned. In 1550, at the suggestion of Bindo Altoviti, Michelangelo determined to consecrate himself to this work and had almost persuaded Julius III, but the money was lacking.[16] In 1559 the Florentines took up the idea again and decided to put a church of a new plan on the old foundations, and their procurators, Francesco Bandini, Uberto Ubaldini and Tommaso de' Bardi, asked Michelangelo to take charge of it in spite of his duties at St. Peter's. Cosmo de' Medici himself wrote a most flattering letter begging him to accept, and Michelangelo answered the duke that he "considered his wish an order" and had already shown the Florentine deputies several drawings, of which they had chosen the one which he considered the best.[17] "I am

[16] Letters of Michelangelo to Vasari, August 1—October 13, 1550.
[17] Letter of Michelangelo to Cosmo, November, 1559.

sorry," he added, "to be now so old and so little alive that I can not do all I would or all that is my duty to your lordship and the people. Nevertheless I will make the effort by directing everything from my house to accomplish what your lordship desires."[18]

In spite of his age he began with the same enthusiasm with which he had undertaken the unlucky façade of S. Lorenzo. He told the commission that if they carried out his plans "neither the Greeks nor the Romans would have done anything like it." "Words," says Vasari, "of a kind that never came from the mouth of Michelangelo before or after, for he was extremely modest."

The Florentines accepted his plans without change and gave the execution of them to Tiberio Calcagni.

"Michelangelo," says Vasari, "explained his project to Tiberio so that he could make a clear and accurate drawing of it. He gave him the profiles of the interior and exterior and made him a model in wax. Tiberio in ten days finished a model two feet high, and as it pleased all the people another model was made in wood which is now in the Consulate. It is a work of such rare art that there never was seen a church so beautiful, so rich and with such variety of fancy." The building was commenced and five thousand crowns spent; then the money gave out and the work stopped, to Michelangelo's most profound disappointment. Not only was the church not built, but the model disappeared with all the plans. This was the last artistic disappointment of his life.[19]

He could no longer paint, but he still continued to work

[18] Letter of Michelangelo to Cosmo, November 1, 1559. The same, November 1, 1559, and March 5, 1560.

[19] Michelangelo in the last period of his life, when he seemed entirely devoted to architecture and poetry, and many other ambitious plans, like that of continuing the arcade of the Loggia dei Lanzi around the palace of the Signory at Florence, of connecting

at his sculpture from a sort of physical need. Vasari says that "his genius and strength could not live without creation." He attacked a block of marble to cut from it four figures larger than life, of which one was a dead Christ.[20] He did this to amuse himself and to pass the time, and because he said that work with a chisel kept him in health. He worked at night[21] and slept very little, and had made himself a helmet of cardboard to hold a lighted candle on his head so that with both hands free he could light what he was doing. Even at that age he cut the marble with such impetuosity and vigour that it seemed to fly in pieces. He broke off in one blow great fragments four or five inches thick and left a line so pure that if he had gone a hair's-breadth further he would have risked ruining the whole. This did happen to many of his works, which remained merely blocked out like the figures in the Boboli grotto, or half finished like the Madonna of the Medici chapel, or destroyed, as all but happened to the admirable Descent from the Cross in the cathedral at Florence.

"He would break a work in pieces," says Vasari, "either because the block was hard and full of flaws and sparks shot out from under the chisel, or because the uncompromising judgment of this man was never contented with anything that he did, which is easily proved by the fact

---

the Farnese palace and the Farnesina by a bridge, of raising in the court of the Belvedere a Moses striking water from the rock, etc. It was that taste for the colossal, and what we might even dare to call the uselessly colossal, which was handed down through his school as far as Bernini.

[20] In 1553. See Condivi. This is the famous Pietà of the cathedral of Florence. Blaise de Vigenère in "Les Images de Philostrate," Paris, 1629, speaks of a Pietà on which Michelangelo was working in 1550 for his own tomb.

[21] All his life he suffered from insomnia brought on by overwork, a fever which continually consumed him and his ascetic sobriety.

that so few of the works of his maturity are complete; the only finished ones dated from his youth."

The Florentine sculptor Tiberio Calcagni, who was a friend as well as his assistant at S. Giovanni dei Fiorentini, found the debris of a Pietà one day, and asked why he had destroyed "so admirable a work." Michelangelo told him that it was partly the fault of his servant Urbino, who urged him every day to finish it, when he was already annoyed by a flaw in the marble so that he had lost patience and had broken it. He would have destroyed it entirely but that his servant Antonio "had begged for what remained." Tiberio bought the marble from Antonio for two hundred gold crowns and asked Michelangelo's permission to finish it for their mutual friend Francesco Bandini. Michelangelo was entirely willing, and the group was restored by Tiberio, who completed several parts of it, but Bandini, Michelangelo and Tiberio all died and it was never finished.[22]

It is all the more moving for that reason. In the half-shadow behind the high altar in Florence it stirs one with indescribable emotion. Perhaps no other work of Michelangelo is so human or speaks so directly to the soul. "From heart to heart," as Beethoven wrote at the end of his mass in D. It is the expression of those long nights when he was alone face to face with his sorrow and spoke only to himself. He represents himself in the form of an old man, in a monk's cowl, bending with infinite sadness and tenderness to support the sinking body of the dead Christ.

In this piece of stone hardly blocked out smoulders deep sorrow and an agony of pain. But what great love is in that suffering, in the scarcely modelled face of the

[22] Two other unfinished Pietàs have been preserved. One is in the court of the Rondanini palace in Rome, the other has just been found in Palestrina.

mother with closed eyes and parted lips, and in the tender movement of the hand which rests on the naked breast of her son, whose head has sunk against her shoulder. How much Michelangelo has softened since his early work, how far this feeling is from the implacable heroism of his youth, how far it is indeed from the lovely Pietà of St. Peter's, where serene beauty rises above the sorrow. Here he suffers and abandons himself to the suffering. What matters a lack of proportion and an uncertain composition?[23] The work is unique in its intimacy. It is his whole soul laid bare.

Michelangelo never lacked illustrious friends. From the time of his early youth, when he talked in the gardens of San Marco with Lorenzo de' Medici and Poliziano, he was always in close touch with the best among the nobles and princes, prelates and poets and artists of Italy.[24] He had a peculiarly close friendship with Francesco Berni and Sebastiano del Piombo[25] under Clement VII and with Luigi del Riccio, Donato Giannotti and Benedetto Varchi[26] under Paul III, and at the close of his life he was

[23] The figures are not on the same scale, especially the figure of the Magdalen, which is too small. She is colder than the rest of the group and more finished, and we may suspect that it was upon her figure that Calcagni worked.

[24] Among these artists he knew particularly well Francesco Grannacci, Giuliano Bugiardini, Jacopo Sansovino, Aristotele da San Gallo, Rosso, Pontormo, Guglielmo della Porta, Vignole, and the musician Archadelt.

[25] Correspondence between Sebastiano del Piombo and Michelangelo has been published by Gaetano Milanesi with a French translation by A. LePileur and an introduction by E. Müntz. in the Bibl. internationale de l'Art (Librairie de l'Art, 1890).

[26] Donato Giannotti has, as we have said, preserved the memory of these relations in his "Dialoghi," 1545. Michelangelo was particularly intimate with Luigi del Riccio through their mutual friendship with the beautiful Cecchino dei Bracci, whose premature death in 1544 inspired Michelangelo with a cycle of verses.

surrounded by the pious worship of pupils and admirers like Benvenuto Cellini, Bronzino, Daniele da Volterra, Leone Leoni, Vasari and his biographer, almost his hagiographer, Condivi, whose book begins with these words:

"Since the hour when our Lord God by special mercy judged me worthy to not only see Michelangelo, which I could hardly have dared to hope for, but to enjoy his affection, his conversation and his confidence—grateful for such a great blessing, I have made all possible effort not only to collect and write down the instructions which he gave me on art, but all his words, actions and habits and all things in his life which seemed to me worthy of praise, admiration or emulation. This I do to pay back a little of the infinite obligation which I owe to him no less than to be useful to others by giving them the example of such a man."[27]

The artists were not the only ones who looked upon Michelangelo as a supernatural being, for princes bowed before his fame and his great virtue as Vasari calls it. Cosmo de' Medici, who tried in vain to recall him to Florence, even offering to make him a senator,[28] treated Michelangelo as an equal. Cosmo's son Don Francesco received him with even greater respect (in October, 1561), his cap in his hand "showing a reverence without limit for so extraordinary a man."

In spite of all this adulation, or perhaps because of it, he had as little intercourse as possible with the world. Popes and princes, men of letters and artists, held but

---

[27] "La Vita Michelangelo," by Ascanio Condivi, appeared in July, 1553, in Rome, published by Antonio Blado and dedicated to Julius III. The first edition of Vasari's "Vite" had already appeared in 1551 and Vasari had sent it to Michelangelo, who had thanked him in the sonnet "Se con lo stile."

[28] See Benvenuto Cellini.

small place in his life, except a few favourite pupils like Vasari, for whom he showed a fatherly affection, especially in his last years, when, growing more feeble day by day, he grew more demonstrative.

"I have been to see my great Michelangelo," Vasari wrote to Cosmo in 1560. "He did not expect me and showed as much feeling as a father who has recovered a lost son. He threw his arms around my neck and kissed me a thousand times, crying with pleasure" (lacrymando per dolcezza).[29]

But the best of his heart was kept for his kin and for a few humble friends. Of his two remaining brothers, Giovan Simone died in 1548, and Gismondo, with whom he had never had much intercourse, in 1555. He turned to Lionardo and Francesca, the children of his favourite brother Buonarroto, for the family affection which he could not do without. He charged himself with the education of Lionardo, who was nine years old at his father's death, and the long correspondence between them which has been preserved shows how seriously he took his responsibility as guardian. The children grew up and after they had married he found himself even more lonely than before.[30]

In his own house he had assistants who were devoted to him, but of no great ability. "He had trouble with those in his service," says Vasari, "for he never chanced to find men who could imitate him well." Pietro Urbano de Pistoia was intelligent, but would take no trouble; Antonio Mini was willing, but not intelligent; and Ascanio

[29] Letter of Vasari to Cosmo de' Medici, April 8, 1560. See also the affectionate letter of Michelangelo to Sebastiano del Piombo in May, 1555.

[30] Francesca married, in 1538, Michele de Niccolo Guicciardini. Lionardo married, in 1553, Cassandra, the daughter of Donato Ridolfi.

della Ripa Transone tried hard, but never succeeded in doing anything. It is possible that he deliberately chose mediocre assistants in order to have docile tools instead of collaborators, which indeed would have been quite legitimate; but Condivi says that it is not true that he refused to teach them, but, on the contrary, he did so willingly. "I myself am the proof of that, for he opened the secrets of his heart to me. The trouble was that he met with pupils that had no ability, or with able ones who were not persevering and who after a few months of his teaching thought themselves already masters. And though he took a great deal of trouble to help them he did not want to have this known, for he loved rather to do good than to seem to do it."

His letters show what fatherly patience he had with these poor creatures. He forgave them any folly if they only showed a little good will and affection.

The one that he cared for the most was Francesco d'Amadore, called Urbino, the son of Guido di Colonello de Castel Durante, who was in his service from 1530 and had worked on the tomb of Julius II. Michelangelo was worried about what would become of Urbino after his own death, and one day, says Vasari, he asked him, "What will you do when I die?" When Urbino answered, "I will have to serve some other master," Michelangelo said, "Poor fellow, I am going to cure your poverty," and gave him two thousand crowns on the spot, "a gift such as only emperors and popes bestow."

It was Urbino who died first in 1555, and the day after Michelangelo wrote to his nephew Lionardo: "I must tell you that Urbino died yesterday at ten o'clock. He has left me so sad and troubled because of the love I had for him that it would have been easier to have died with him. He was a worthy man, loyal and faithful. Since he has gone

I do not seem to be alive and I can not recover my peace of mind."[31]

Lionardo and his wife Cassandra, anxious on account of his great grief, went to Rome and found him much weakened. But he drew new energy from the charge which Urbino had left him in the guardianship of his sons, one of whom was his godson and bore his name. He wrote to Cornelia, Urbino's wife, that he would like to take the little Michelangelo to live with him. He showed him more affection than even the children of his nephew, and had him taught all that Urbino had wished him to learn.[32]

He showed the most touching affection for his old servants, and also for those of his family whom he had taken in after his father's death, and for the workmen who had helped him at Carrara and in the Sistine Chapel.

His enemies accused him of avarice,[33] but Vasari answers the charge with indignation and a list of his royal

---

[31] A few days before Michelangelo had lost his last brother, Gismondo. See also his admirable letter to Vasari, February 23, 1556.

[32] Letter of Michelangelo to Cornelia, March 28, 1557. He quarrelled with Cornelia in 1559, when she married again, and wanted to take the charge of the children from her, but their friendship was re-established in 1561.

[33] He justified these accusations by his almost sordid manner of living and constant complaints of poverty, although he was really rich. A Denunzia de' beni, in 1534, before he had received anything from Paul III, showed that he owned a house and three estates in Settignano, a property at St. Stephano de Pozzolatico, two farms and a house at Stradello, a farm at Rovezzano, three houses in the Via Ghibellina, one house in the Via Mozza, etc. The inventory made after his death in Rome showed seven or eight hundred gold crowns (worth about four to five thousand francs) and Vasari tells us that he had twice given his nephew Lionardo seven thousand crowns, beside two thousand to Urbino and sums invested at Florence.

gifts to all his friends: "To Messer Tommaso dei Cavalieri, to Messer Bindo Altoviti, and Fra Bastiano (del
Piombo) drawings of great value. To Antonio Mini all
the drawings, cartoons and models in wax and clay and
the painting of Leda; to Gherardo Perini some divinely
beautiful heads drawn in pencil which passed later into
the hands of Don Francesco, Prince of Florence, who
rightly esteemed them among his treasures; to Bartolommeo Bettini a cartoon of Venus with Cupid kissing her, a
divine work now in possession of his heirs in Florence; to
the Marchese del Vasto a cartoon of the *noli me tangere*,
a beautiful work from which Pontormo made a painting
as he did from the Venus and Cupid; to Roberto Strozzi
the two Slaves in marble; to his servant Antonio and to
Francesco Bandini the Pietà in marble which he broke. I
do not understand how a man can be called avaricious
who gives away such works of art worth many thousands
of crowns."

His generosity was not limited to his friends, for he
gave much to the poor, especially the disreputable poor.
He particularly remembered poor young girls and dowered
them secretly, taking care that they should never know
the name of their benefactor.

He was always ailing in health, and several times very
near death, particularly in 1544, when he was nursed by
his friend Riccio in the house of the Strozzi, and in his
later years he suffered cruelly from gout and stone. His
indomitable nervous energy supported him, and at eighty-
five he inspected the works of St. Peter's on horseback. In
spite of a severe attack of gout in August, 1561, he would
let no one take care of him and he still lived alone. His
nephew Lionardo was least of all allowed to interfere with
these arrangements, for Michelangelo attributed his anx-
iety to an interest in his inheritance and did not hesitate
to tell him so.

Both the Duke of Tuscany and the pope were anxious about the plans and drawings of his public works, which Michelangelo kept in his own house, for fear that they might be stolen after his death. So in June, 1563, at the instigation of Vasari, who saw that Michelangelo was failing rapidly, Cosmo de' Medici secretly directed his ambassador, Averado Serristori, to keep a strict watch on the domestic life of Michelangelo and on everyone who came to his house. In case of his sudden death an inventory was to be taken of all his possessions, drawings, cartoons, models, silver, etc., and a watch to be kept that nothing was taken in the first confusion. All that had to do with the construction of St. Peter's or the sacristy or the Laurentian library was to be put carefully aside.

Weakened as he was, Michelangelo still worked. Since 1562 he had hardly written at all himself, and Daniele da Volterra did most of his correspondence, but he never relinquished his chisel. On February 12, 1564, he spent the whole day standing at work on his Pietà, and on the fourteenth, although he was seized with fever, he rode out on horseback into the country in the rain, and would not consent to stay in his bed until the sixteenth.

On the eighteenth of February he died in full consciousness, with Daniele da Volterra and his faithful friend Tommaso dei Cavalieri beside him.

> Giunto è gia' l corso della vita mia
> Con tempestoso mar per fragil barca
> Al comus porto. . . .[34]

Cosmo de' Medici was at once notified by his ambassador, and the next day the governor of Rome made an

[34] Now hath my life across a stormy sea
Like a frail bark reached that wide port where all
Are bidden. . . .

(J. A. Symonds' translation.)

inventory of Michelangelo's property in the presence of Pier Luigi Gaeta and Cavalieri. There was much less than had been expected, for he had burned almost all his drawings. They found a chest containing seven or eight thousand crowns and a trunk closed and sealed and full of papers, and also three statues, the unfinished Pietà,[35] a figure of Saint Peter just begun, and a little unfinished figure of Christ bearing the cross in the style of that in the Minerva, and yet different. There were besides ten cartoons as follows:

1. The plan of St. Peter's.
2. The façade of a palace (a small cartoon).
3. A window of St. Peter's.
4. The old plan for St. Peter's, after a drawing of San Gallo's.
5. Three sketches of little figures.
6. Windows.
7. A Pietà, merely sketched. A composition of nine figures.
8. Three large figures and two *putti*.
9. Large figure (a study of an apostle for the figure of Saint Peter).
10. Farewell of Christ to his mother, drawn for Cardinal Morone.[36]

This last drawing was given to Cavalieri as Michelangelo had wished. The rest went to Lionardo, who reached Rome three days after his uncle's death, and who acquired also some little sketches which Michelangelo had given to Michele Alberti and Jacopo del Duca—an annunciation and a prayer at Gethsemane. These show how much the thought of the gospel filled Michelangelo's mind.[37]

---

[35] The Pietà Rondanini.
[36] Gotti, Vol. II, p. 358.
[37] Besides these there were in the atelier in Florence in the Via

On February 19th Michelangelo's body was carried by the brotherhood to which he belonged, the Confratelli di S. Giovanni Pecolla, to the church of the SS. Apostoli for the funeral mass. The pope had meant to have the body placed in St. Peter's, but Michelangelo had expressed a desire to return to Florence dead, as he could not do so living,[38] and Lionardo was determined to carry out his last wishes in accordance with the orders of Cosmo de' Medici, who promised to erect a statue to him in the Florentine cathedral. The Romans would not allow the body to be taken away, so it was necessary to wrap it secretly in a roll of cloth and to send it to Florence on the twenty-ninth as merchandise.

Thus did Michelangelo return to his country on March 10, 1564. The next day the artists of Florence carried his body by torchlight to the church of Santa Croce. The crowd was so great that they could hardly force their way through the church. In the sacristy Vincenzo Borghini, Director of the Florentine Academy of Painters, had the coffin opened. The body was intact and Michelangelo seemed asleep. He was dressed in black velvet, a felt hat on his head, and on his feet boots and spurs, just as while living he had had the habit of sleeping, dressed and ready to rise and take up his work.[39]

The Academy of Florence had been preparing since

Mozza a number of blocks of marble and the beautiful statue of Victory intended for the tomb of Julius II, and which in 1565 was taken to the Palazzo Vecchio. Also Antonio del Franzese, Michelangelo's servant, who was with him at the time of his death, gave to the Duke of Urbino in 1570 a statuette of Moses which his master had given to him.

[38] Gaye, "Carteggio inedito d'artisti," 1839, Vol. III, p. 131.

[39] The Florentine Academy of Painters had just been founded in 1563, and Michelangelo had been unanimously chosen as a president together with Cosmo de' Medici, January 31, 1563.

March 2d for the solemn obsequies. Varchi was given the
funeral oration, Bronzino, Vasari, Cellini and Ammanati
the artistic arrangements. On the 14th of July, 1564, in
the church of S. Lorenzo, a triumphant memorial service
was held in the presence of a hundred artists and an innumerable crowd of people.[40]

Between the two side doors arose a huge catafalque.
Daniele da Volterra had wanted to use for the tomb the
fine Victory and other sculptures of the Via Mozza, but
this most reverent and appropriate idea for the glorification of the master was not accepted.[41] Instead, a huge
arrangement, disproportionate and swollen, was erected,
a real tower of Babel to which each sculptor of Florence
brought his stone. It was undoubtedly, however, a fine
thought to associate all the world of artists in a supreme
homage to the man whom Italy considered the incarnation
of her genius and the God himself of art.[42] The result of
these combined efforts was only to prove more strikingly
the contrast between the man who was dead and the men
who claimed the right to succeed him. The agglomeration
of sculpture recalls also that bitter saying of Michelangelo
shortly before his end that "art and death do not go well
together."

"L'arte e la morte non va bene insieme."

From 1564 to 1572 Vasari raised in Santa Croce, at
the expense of Lionardo Buonarroti, and with the col-

---

[40] The Duke was not there, Cellini was ill and could not come
and Francesco da San Gallo did not appear.

[41] Daniele da Volterra had offered to make a sketch for the
tomb with his assistant, Jacopo del Duca, but Vasari's jealousy
prevented it. Daniele died April 4, 1566, after having made rough
models for three busts of Michelangelo which Jacopo del Duca
or Michele Alberti finished after him.

[42] See the detailed account of the obsequies; "Esequie del
divino Michelangelo," Florence, Giunti, 1564. Varchi wrote the
"Orazione funerale."

laboration of Borghini, Valerio Cioli and Battista Lorenzi, the monument to Michelangelo. Thode has proved that the so-called tomb of Michelangelo in the SS. Apostoli in Rome has nothing whatever to do with him. It is really the monument of a professor of medicine, Ferdinando Eustacio, and the false attribution dates only from 1823.

Chapter 6

The Genius of Michelangelo and His Influence on Italian Art

"I HAVE NO FRIEND of any kind," said Michelangelo in 1509, "and I do not want any."[1]

Forty years later, in 1548, Michelangelo wrote again, "I am always alone and I speak to no one."[2]

"From his youth," says Condivi, "Michelangelo had consecrated himself not only to sculpture and painting, but to all the other arts with such devouring energy that he had to separate himself almost entirely from the society of men. For that reason many people considered him proud, and others eccentric or mad. In reality it was his love of work alone, his labour without respite, which made him solitary, for he was so filled by the joy and rapture which his work gave him that the society of men did not offer him any pleasure, but rather bored him by distracting

[1] Letter of October, 1509.
[2] Letter of March, 1548, to Lionardo Buonarroto.

him from his own thoughts. Like the great Scipio, he was never less lonely than when he was alone."

That passionate solitude was the very soul of the genius and of the work of Michelangelo. He lived shut up in himself without any real connection with the art of his time. He despised Raphael because he said, "All his talent came from study and not from nature."[3] He himself declared that he derived all his inspiration from within, and if in his pride he underestimated what he was always studying with feverish and persistent ardour, yet it is true that he never sought in the study of the works of others a means of changing or of renewing his own personality, but only of still further emphasising it. In a way he sought from others not examples or lessons, but reasons for being still more himself. It is true that from the beginning to the end he fed on his own soul. Who knows the man, knows his work.

The most striking thing about this extraordinarily unified nature is that it was composed of hostile worlds; a brutal materialism and serene idealism, an infatuation with pagan strength and beauty and a Christian mysticism; a mixture of physical violence and intellectual abstraction; a platonic soul in an athlete's body. That indissoluble union of opposing forces which undoubtedly caused part of his suffering was also the cause of his unique greatness. We feel that the supreme balance of his art is the result of a fierce struggle, and it is the sense of that struggle which gives to the work its heroic character. All is passion even to the abstract idea, so that idealism, which with many artists is a cause of coldness and death, is here a hearth burning with love and hate.[4]

There is undoubtedly a danger in that mystic faith

[3] Condivi.
[4] See the *Lezione* of Benedetto Varchi on the sonnet of Michelangelo, "Non ha l'ottimo Artista. . . ."

which loses itself in inward visions of such charm that they often leave a feeling of only disgust and contempt for reality.

> Non vider gli occhi mei cosa mortale
>
> .   .   .   .   .
>
> E se creata a Dio non fusse eguale
> Altro che l bel di fuor, ch' à gl'occhi piace,
> Piu non vorria; ma perch' è si fallace,
> Tracende nella forma universale.[5]

Varchi was quite right in recognising in Michelangelo the Socratic spirit.[6] Whether he gained these ideas from the teaching of the great Platonists with whom he had talked as a youth in the gardens of San Marco or whether that teaching had merely revealed to him his true nature there is certainly a close relationship between the theories on art of the school of Socrates and those of Michelangelo.

Parrhasius believed in representing only "the perspective, the light and the shadow, the softness, hardness and surface of bodies." Socrates taught him that the object of painting is to represent the soul and the innermost being.[7] "The fields and trees can teach me nothing," he says in the "Phædo"; "I only find what is useful to me among men in the towns." These very men only interested him

---

[5] I saw no mortal beauty with these eyes
     When perfect peace in thy fair eyes I found;
     But far within, where all is holy ground,
   My soul felt love, her comrade of the skies;
   For she was born with God in Paradise;
     Else should we still to transient love be bound;
     But, finding these so false, we pass beyond,
   Unto the Love of loves that never dies.
                          (Translation of J. A. Symonds.)
[6] "*Tutti i componimenti di lui pieni d'amore Socratico, e di concetti Platonici.*"
[7] Xenophon, Memor, Vol. III, p. 10.

because there was something eternal in them. The fugitive and changing side of their physiognomy, which for us makes the delicate charm of life and the object of painting, seemed to him an empty and wearisome illusion. Art creates illusions. The objects which it represents are "the dreams of the human imagination offered to people who can see. It is an image which one shows in the distance to little children who can not reason, in order to create illusions for them. These illusions of the senses distract the soul from the only realities, eternal ideas."

Michelangelo reasoned thus in his disdain of all exact reproduction of nature. He had studied it with passion but, in order to discover its laws, he regarded it as an enemy which held the human spirit prisoner. He wanted to free himself from it, he wanted to make of it an instrument for his thought. That is why he sought for and discovered its machinery, and when he could guide it at will he outraged it; he made it produce unprecedented results. He constructed for himself out of his profound knowledge of anatomy a general idea of man, and thereafter, without having recourse to any observation of individuals, he recreated the whole of nature in the image of his ideas and in the likeness of God, source and originator of ideas.

> Come dal foco 'l cald' 'esser' diviso
> Nom puo 'l bel dall' eterno; e la mia stima
> Esalta che ne scende, e chi 'l somiglia.

"As heat can not be separated from fire, so beauty can not be from eternity; and my thought extols what comes from it and what resembles it."

He wanted to express in his work only what was eternal, and he did not believe he could do this with external objects. He tried, therefore, to give to everything he did a character of compelling force. His Platonic idealism was

lined with Christian pessimism. Like Vittoria Colonna, he
was filled with the sense of the beauty of all human things,
and he was obsessed with the idea of death.

He lived in an exhausted epoch which no longer had
any happy sense of reality. In God was the only help, in
the eternal and immutable perfection. Michelangelo was
filled with dislike for all realism. Like Plato, he despised
painting in comparison with sculpture.

"Painting seems to me the better the more it resembles
sculpture, and the sculpture worse the more it resembles
painting. Sculpture is the torch of painting, and between
the two there is the same difference as between the sun
and the moon."[8]

If he was above all things a sculptor it was because he
found in sculpture the most appropriate expression of his
abstract and concentrated genius.

> Non ha l'ottimo artista alcun concetto,
> Ch' un marmo solo in se non circonscriva
> Col suo soverchio, et solo à quello arriva
> La man, che ubbidisce all' intelleto.[9]

Moreover he reduced sculpture to its most simple form,
the isolated statue. Michelangelo had little liking for bas-
reliefs and groups, which he hardly ever made, and where
he always shows some awkwardness. What we know,

---

[8] He adds: "He who wrote that painting was nobler than sculpture, if that idea is a sample of his intelligence, then my servant
knows more than he does."
This seems to be directed at Lionardo. See the first chapter of
"Trattato della Pittura."

[9] The best of artists hath no thought to show
  Which the rough stone in its superfluous shell
  Doth not include; to break the marble spell
Is all the hand that serves the brain can do.

(Translation of J. A. Symonds.)

through Cellini and Vasari, of his manner of working would incline us to feel to-day that the basis of his sculpture and of all his art was drawing,[10] because that was most immaterial and closest to the form of his thought.

No one has ever drawn as Michelangelo did, and Charles Blanc is right in saying that "if he is unequal in his sculptures and his frescoes, never does his drawing, even when apparently most careless and most summary, betray any feebleness of hand or distraction or hesitancy of spirit." Not only do we penetrate, then, into the mystery of his creativeness, into the dreams and soliloquies of his lonely soul, but we discover there also his most intimate and perfect expression. There he is altogether himself, as Beethoven is in his quartets and in his short pieces for the piano.[11]

I compare these two purposely; for the genius of each of them was solitary, intellectual and passionate, only realising itself completely in the most simple and abstract

[10] If it is true that Michelangelo attacked the marble with the greatest fury, it was only after he had prepared his drawings and his models with the most minute care. Cellini in his "Trattati dell' oreficeria" (Florence, 1557) says that for the statues in the Sacristy of S. Lorenzo he saw him first make models of the same height as the statue was to be and then draw with charcoal on the marble the general appearance of his figure. Vasari says almost the same thing in regard to the four statues of Captives sketched in the block and not yet cut from it.

[11] The science of design or drawing, said Michelangelo, according to the Dialogues of Francis of Holland, is the source and the essence of painting, of sculpture, of architecture and of all kinds of representation as well as the soul of all the sciences (Third Part of the "Dialogues sur la Peinture dans la Ville de Rome"). "Sculpture," says Francis of Holland, "is clearly bound to drawing; it comes out of it and at bottom is nothing more than the drawing itself. The great draughtsman, Michelangelo, said to me many times that he regarded it as a greater thing to make a masterly stroke with the pen than with the chisel." (Ibid., Second Part.)

forms in which the senses had the least part and the spirit the greatest. All the voluptuous charm of art was not only foreign to Michelangelo, but antagonistic to him. The more art was aimed at the senses the more he despised it.

> Voglia sfrenata el senso è, non amore,
> Che l'alma uccide. . . .[12]

Painting, therefore, seemed to him, as it did to Plato, less virile and less pure than sculpture, because of its seductive quality, its illusive magic which imitates the appearance of things and merely creates illusions. He disdained it inasmuch as it appealed through the attraction of colours at the expense of the idea. He could not endure painting in oils, which he said was only good for women.[13] He rejected landscape, and like Plato only saw in it a vague and deceiving illusion—a sport for children and ignorant people. He had a horror of portraits. They seemed to him a form of flattery for the gratification of vain curiosity and the imperfect illusion of the senses.[14] It is curious to contrast with these principles which were adopted by a part of the Italian school in the sixteenth century, the naïve confession of faith of Dürer at almost the same period. "The art of painting is used in the service of the Church to show the sufferings of Christ and of

[12] Sense is not love, but lawlessness accursed;
   This kills the soul. . . .
                              (Translation of J. A. Symonds.)
[13] "Or for sluggards like Sebastiano del Piombo." He had a quarrel because of this remark with Sebastiano, who tried to persuade him to paint the Last Judgment in oils.
[14] "Aborriva il fare somigliare al vivo" (Vasari).—"Michelangelo never would paint a portrait."—(Journal de Bernin, Gazette des Beaux Arts, Vol. XVII, p. 358.) "His rule," says Vasari, "was never to make any likeness of a living person unless he was of transcendent beauty."

many other models of virtue, and it also preserves the faces of men after their death." (1513)

That pious and bourgeois realism of Germany and Flanders filled Michelangelo with the same sort of contempt that many artists of to-day feel for subject-painting. "It is," he says, "an anecdotal and sentimental art, which aims only at success and obtains it easily, not by its own value, but by the choice of its subjects. These are pious figures for which tears are always ready, or else rags, ruins, very green fields shaded by trees, rivers and bridges —what they call landscapes—with many figures here and there. That sort of thing is always popular; the least artistic spirit can find something there that appeals to it; it is enough to be inquisitive and to have good eyes." Again—"Flemish painting seems beautiful to women, especially to those who are either old or very young, and to monks and nuns and to a few people of quality who are deaf to true harmony. Although it makes a good effect in the eyes of some people, in truth there is neither reason nor art in it, no proportion, no symmetry, no selection, and no grandeur. In fact, such painting is without body or vigour. The only real paintings are those done in Italy. These are not, like the Flemish pictures, made for the pious.[15] They will never cause anyone to shed a tear."[16]

We can well understand that disdainful confession of faith. What artist is there who has not felt this same irritation at the success of mediocre work exploited by the

[15] "Flemish painting generally is more pleasing to the devout than Italian painting."

[16] Francis of Holland, "Quatre Entretiens sur la Peinture," held in Rome in 1538–1539, written in 1548, published by Joachim de Vasconcellos (translation into French in "Les Arts en Portugal," by Comte Raczynski, Paris, Renouard, 1844). To prove the theory of Michelangelo, Vittoria Colonna, who presided over this talk, undertook the defense of the religious and consolatory art of the North.

sentimentality of an uncritical public and who will not understand Michelangelo's haughty refusal to share this too easy success? This pride, ennobling as it is to the character, is unfortunately perilous for art; it cuts it off from all simple souls, it isolates it in the arrogant feeling of inner perfection and of a secret ideal which very few can know or understand. As Michelangelo says:

"Good painting is noble and devout in itself, for among the wise nothing tends more to elevate the soul or to raise it toward devotion than the difficulty of that perfection which approaches God and becomes one with him. Good painting is but a copy of this perfection, a shadow of his pencil, a music, a melody, and only a very keen intelligence can feel the difficulty of it. That is why it is so rare and why so few people can attain to it or know how to produce it. Painting is the music of God, the inner reflection of his luminous perfection."[17]

If instead of Michelangelo with his ardent faith and that warmth of enthusiasm which sweeps along his idealism and makes of the Divine Idea as he conceives it a living being to whom he passionately desires to unite himself we should take, I do not say a sceptic or an atheist, but a sincere believer after the manner of the Council of Trent, a Vasari or a Zucchero, then God will be to them not a source of love and ecstasy, but the principle of reason. The reason of the wise—behold the beginning and the end of art. A hundred years after Michelangelo, Poussin was to bind all art in obedience to this principle. He applied all its natural resources to the rendering of one idea. With him the attention is confined to the idea of the work— that is the principal thing. The abstract idea is more important than the form; thought alone is spontaneous; all

[17] We find the same ideas, more exuberant and more confused, in the writings of Lomazzo, "Idea del Tempio della Pittura" (1590).

the rest—life, expression, colour—is determined by the logic of reason. The subject regulates the composition and determines the centre of interest and the groupings of the picture; it indicates the character of the people, their moral aspect and, consequently, their exterior, for the two are bound together. It determines the character of the landscape, which must bear a logical relationship to the scene; it presides even over the execution of the work. The manner of painting is imposed by the subject to be treated; it will be Phrygian or Dorian or Lydian, according to whether the idea is gentle or serious or sad. In this way everything is logical and calculated. Michelangelo's mystical ardour toward divine perfection at least left him his impetuous liberty of feeling. Poussin no longer left anything to chance. His reason commanded and his hand obeyed. If I name him here it is because he was both the end and the climax of artistic intellectualism. At least Poussin left on his work the impress of his great intelligence. His system rests on this idea, and with him the idea was clear and powerful. But what would it be in the hands of men of mediocre talent? The number of artists who either think for themselves, or express with new force the ideas of others, is infinitesimal. Moreover, the ideal is ordinarily to them merely an emphatic rendering of a vague conception of perfection which they have been taught. Under pretext of an intellectual ideal they deform nature; they leave it little by little, turning their backs, their eyes proudly closed, looking only within themselves. "La bellezza," says Tomazzo, "e lontana dala materia" (Beauty is far from matter).[18] The symbol of the period which was to follow is that very Lomazzo,[19] painter, æsthetician—blind.

[18] Idea del Tempio, etc.
[19] Lomazzo became blind when he was twenty-three, but that did not prevent him from judging of painters and their works until his death when over sixty.

Blind, more or less, were all who lived around Michelangelo. Their too feeble eyes were dazzled by this sun which shone alone in that twilight of art, the night which was falling on Italy of the Renaissance. A long time after that sun had disappeared below the horizon the radiant glow still remained in the sky. Michelangelo enthralled Italian art.

There is no comparison between the influence which he exerted and that of the other masters of the sixteenth century, Corregio and Raphael. However superior they may have been to their century, Corregio and Raphael only reflected its thoughts with more charm and grandeur. Michelangelo is outside of his time, alone, apart and colossal. He is like a great mountain which inspires in those who dwell at the foot an invincible desire to reach the top; and what men have ever existed who were less capable of climbing those austere and sublime heights? All those effeminate artists of the decadence, intoxicated by his inspiration, attempted to express heroic ideas in their insipid works. They lost the sense of proportion which alone could have saved them. Instead of confining themselves to the little world of their own fancy which, though cold, could have been redeemed by sincerity, they attempted great subjects. A mass of forms, heroic figures and furious gestures that they had learned, were whirled about in their mind, uncontrolled either by greatness of intelligence or of heart.

We must remember that Michelangelo lived through more than fifty years of the Golden Age of Italian art and, as happened in our own day to Victor Hugo, admiration for his works increased in proportion as they deserved it less. Even the factions that had been longest hostile to him—the school of Raphael, for instance—recognised his triumph. Perino del Vaga admits that all the painters worshipped him as their master, their leader and the god of drawing.[20]

The independents, or those who boasted that they were, said as Cellini did in his sonnets:

"Just a leaf from thy crown, O divine Michelangelo, who alone art rich, who alone art immortal. That will suffice me and I shall have no desire for anything else, since for me that only is good and beautiful."

Florence, his own country, more even than the rest of Italy gave him blind admiration. The Academy of Drawing, founded by Vasari, was a college of disciples and apostles. Since Michelangelo's great paintings were at Rome the Florentines copied chiefly his statues, devoting themselves principally, as Lanzi says, to ostentatiously showing "magna ossa lacertosque."[21]

This was in accordance with the doctrine of the master, who declared that sculpture should be the school of the painter and the ideal of painting. Cellini, thinking to define the thought of Michelangelo, absurdly declares and demonstrates that sculpture is seven times greater than painting.

The painter formed himself from this time on by the study of statues, and especially of those of Michelangelo. Colour was therefore regarded as a secondary consideration,[22] and the only aim pursued was drawing over-ac-

[20] Perino del Vaga made this declaration when he refused to undertake the drawings for the jewel-box of Cosmo de Medici, when he found that they had addressed themselves first to Michelangelo. (Jay, "Receuil de Lettres sur la Peinture." Claude Tolomei à Apoll. Philarète.)

[21] Luigi Lanzi; "Storia Pittorica d'Italia, Bassano, 1795–96," Vol. I, p. 167.

[22] Tintoretto himself, under the influence of Michelangelo, says: "The most beautiful colours are black and white because they give relief to figures by light and shade," and at the end of his life, abandoning the principles of the Venetian School, he gives the preference to drawing, "Draw, draw now and always."

centuated, full of unreasonable action, and of excessive virtuosity. If he seemed to Cellini the greatest painter of all time, it was only because all painting from Cellini's point of view was an imitation of sculpture, and the artist who came nearest to him in perfection is Bronzino.[23]

The danger of following a model is less if the model can be understood, but the ideas of Michelangelo absolutely escaped his admirers. How could it be otherwise when all his work is an act of revolt against his century. We can but smile with pity when we see his contemporaries expressing their enthusiasm for the formidable Night in precious and carefully chosen phrases.[24]

What supreme irony! The world only sees and admires the outer form of those tremendous incarnations of contempt and weariness which are called Moses or the Day, Victory subduing the Prisoner, the Dawn or the Slaves. The world applauds the style of the imprecations launched against it! It even repeats them without knowing the meaning.

Two drawings by Federigo Zucchero, which are in the Louvre, show a number of artists installed in the chapel of S. Lorenzo zealously copying Michelangelo's statues. How many artists of the sixteenth century built their entire

[23] Daniele da Volterra was also more a sculptor than a painter, and ended by giving himself up to sculpture. He made casts of the statues of the Medici and also some statues of his own. Some of his pictures, like the David and Goliath in the Louvre, which is painted on both sides, are only two faces of one of his statues. Rosso and Salviati were also sculptors.

[24] The verses of Giovanni Strozzi (1545) are well known:

La Notte, che tu vedi in si dolci atti
Dormir, fu da un Angelo scolpita
In questo sasso, e perche dorme, ha vita.
Destala, se nol credi, e parleratti.

The night which you see sleeping so peacefully was carved by an angel in this rock. Since she sleeps, she lives. If you do not believe it awake her and she will speak to you.

work on these notes without ever thinking that such forms are only justified by the passions which animate them, and that it is ridiculous to use them as aids to the learned virtuosity of a cold and forced talent!

Battista Franco of Venice, *il Semolei* distinguished himself above all others by his zeal in copying Michelangelo. Vasari says that there was not a sketch, not the roughest note, or any sort of fragment of his which he had not devoutly drawn. He knew the whole Sistine by heart. In 1536 he came to Florence and drew once more all the statues of S. Lorenzo. In 1541 he hurried to Rome for the "première" of the Last Judgment, and he made a drawing of the whole thing "*con infinita maraviglia il designo tutto.*" We can understand that he had no time to do any thinking for himself. For a long time he refrained from painting anything of his own. When he decided to begin it was to reproduce in his Battle of Montemurlo some fragments of the war against Pisa or of the Rape of Ganymede.[25]

The independent Cellini writes in his memoirs: "I devoted myself continually to trying to absorb thoroughly the beautiful style of Michelangelo, and since then I have never departed from it."

A hundred years later still Bernini copied the Last Judgment for two successive years before he began to draw from nature. Scivoli watched him doing it and said: "Sei un furbo; no fai quel che vedi: questa è di Michelangelo." ("You are a fool. You are not drawing what you see; this is nothing but Michelangelo").[26]

Bernini, who tells of this, does not see that it is a criti-

[25] The same thing is true of Girolamo Muziano of Brescia. Even the School of Milan was affected. Lomazzo makes of Michelangelo the ruler of all painting. The imitation of Michelangelo spread especially in sculpture, and there the decadence was dizzying.

[26] "Journal du Voyage du Cavalier Bernin en France," par M. de Chantelou. ("Gazette des Beaux Arts," Vol. XXIX, p. 453.)

cism, for he recommends this same system of education to young artists.

"It is necessary first for a young man to form an idea of the beautiful, for this is of use to him all his life; it ruins young men to begin by drawing from nature, which is almost always weak and mean, and which then fills their imagination, so that they can never produce anything beautiful or great, qualities which are never found in natural things. Those who make use of nature should be already skilful enough to recognise its faults and to correct them. A young man is not capable of this until he has gained full knowledge of beauty."[27]

The essential idea of this teaching was that nature is evil; just what Michelangelo thought. But we now see to what unexpected results his pessimistic idealism led. It produced not only separation from nature, but renunciation of personal feeling for formulas, "since it is not possible for one individual to have light on all subjects nor to grasp without assistance the difficulty of arts so profound and so little understood."

What would Michelangelo have thought of these servile disciples, he who said proudly that "whoever follows others will never go forward, and whoever does not know how to create by his own abilities can gain no profit from the works of other men."

But they had lost even the consciousness of their servility and took more pride in living on Michelangelo's crumbs than he had in creating the work which was to be the nourishment of two centuries. Some drew tranquilly on their memory and their notes, others mimicked the master's grandiose manner, and they were all entirely satisfied with themselves, not one of them realising what their master and model had suffered in giving birth to these works which were so easy for them to imitate.

Michelangelo's idealism had a powerful corrective in "the sense of the beauty of struggle, and the holiness of suffering." "Nothing approaches nearer to God," he wrote, "than the effort to produce a perfect work, because God is perfection."

No one ever struggled more fiercely than this man, who ceaselessly tormented himself and wept at "losing his time uselessly" while he was working at the ceiling of the Sistine Chapel, who wrought with his blood the beings whom he created and was dissatisfied with his sublime creations at the moment of finishing them and left them incomplete, who to his last day in agony and tears

> Piangendo, amando, ardendo, e sospirando,—
> Ch'affetto alcun mortal non mi è più nuovo,—[28]

"Weeping, loving, burning and sighing—for there was no human emotion which he had not felt."

He was vainly seeking the visioned ideal, and in dying he regretted not the joy of living, but his interrupted labours.[29]

Beside that virile modesty what can we think of the absurd vanity of all those little masters who declared that they derived from the great master and believed themselves to be Michelangelos?

[28] Ed. Frey, XLIX.
Michelangelo said one day to Ammanati, "Nelle mie opere caco sangue."
Varchi said to him one day, "Signor Buonarroti, avete il cervello di Giove." Michelangelo answered, "Si vuole il martello di Vulcano per farne uscire qualche cosa." (Quoted by E. Delacroix in his Journal, Vol. II, p. 429.)

[29] Michelangelo said to Cardinal Salviati, who was ministering to him on his death-bed, that he only regretted two things: not to have done all he should have for his salvation, and to be dying just as he was learning the alphabet of his profession. (Journal de Bernin, Vol. XXI, p. 388.)

Vasari dares to write:

"Today art has been brought to such perfection that while our predecessors produced a picture in six years we produce six in one year. I can bear witness since I have seen this done and have done it myself, and nevertheless our works are much more finished and more perfect than those of the renowned painters who preceded us."[30]

Even the weakest ones had the same feeling. Perino del Vaga considered himself very much superior to Masaccio, and in Cellini vanity ended by touching madness. He felt that antiquity was only valuable as a background to his works, and for his Jupiter he used the bronze castings which Primataccio brought from Rome.[31]

When an artist is so sure of success he no longer takes any trouble to deserve it. "Che cartoni o non cartoni," cries Giorlamo da Treviso, "io, io, ho l'arte su la punta dell pennello" ("Have I need of studies, I who have art on the point of my brush!").

The scruples that Michelangelo had felt no longer checked the artists. They were not afraid to finish what they had begun. Pomeranci, Semino, Calvi, painted four square yards a day. Cambiaso painted, at the age of seventeen, the story of Niobe without studies or sketches. He produced as many works as a dozen painters together, and his wife lighted the fire with bundles of drawings which he tossed off every moment. His contemporaries

[30] Vasari, "Vite," Preamble to the Third Part.

Lionardo spent six years in painting some hair, but Corregio only an hour, and with four strokes of his brush gained just the same effect. (Journal de Bernin, Vol. XX, p. 453.)

[31] He went so far as to canonise himself while he was still alive, after a vision in which he saw a miraculous aureole around his own head.

Nothing shows more surely the gulf which separated Michelangelo from his disciples than the comparison of his sombre poetry with the proudly exultant sonnet which serves as preamble to the memoirs of Cellini.

compare him to Michelangelo, and add that the latter does not gain by the comparison. Santi di Tito made a portrait in less than half an hour. He set up a factory in his house and turned them out in enormous quantities. His pupil, Tempesti, did not succeed in finding sufficient occupation for his talents in the great frescoes at Rome and, as a relaxation from painting, made fifteen hundred engravings. In a month Vasari, Tribolo and Andrea del Cosimo built and decorated a palace. In a day Perino del Vaga painted the Passage of the Red Sea.

The Venetians, thanks to their distance from Rome and Florence and to their ardent communion with nature, which to the horror of Vasari they dared to copy honestly,[32] were saved for a time, but in the end caught the infection. The Florentine spirit won this last refuge of art, and Tintoretto infused the spirit of Michelangelo into Venetian realism.[33]

The brain of Italy was a prey to fever.[34] Michelangelo

---

[32] See what Vasari writes of the revolution of Giorgione in 1507 when Giorgione began to "pose before him living and natural things, to represent them as nearly as he could by painting directly with colour without making any drawing." He adds that Giorgione did not perceive that it is necessary, if you wish to arrange and balance a composition, to put it first on paper. "In fact the mind can not very well see or perfectly imagine its own creations, if it does not reveal and explain its thought to the eyes of the body which will aid it in judging—we must add that in drawing on paper one succeeds in filling the mind with beautiful conceptions and learns to make natural objects from memory without being obliged to have them always before you." (Vasari, Ed. 1811, Vol. III, pp. 427–428.) The whole point of view of Florentine art of the sixteenth century is in this naïve avowal.

[33] Tintoretto had long studied Michelangelo. He had brought to him at great expense casts of his statues which Ridolfo says he lighted by a lamp and drew in bold relief. (Ridolfo; "Delle maraviglie dell'arte in Venetia," 1648.)

[34] This fever attacked the art of other countries which were filled with caricatures of Michelangelo, Maarten van Heemskerck,

had destroyed the balance of mind of a period dried out by intellectualism and weakened by the taste for pleasure. The shock of his dazzling light on their eyes, too feeble to bear it, blinded them and inspired a delirium of imagination without poetry, without thought and without life.

The Carracci were needed at the end of the century, if not to snatch Italian art from inevitable death, at least to lend it, emerging from its follies and delusions, an air of dignity and a cold distinction in which it could veil itself to die.

The greatness of Michelangelo was thus fatal to Italian art. So it is with everything that rises too far above its own time. Decadence can only be averted or retarded by intelligent and moderate talents like the Carracci, who, hardly separated from the average of their times, are easily understood by it. They are the geniuses of common sense, and they are, therefore, useful to the common man. The heroes of art are also its tyrants; their glory kills, and the greater they are the more they are to be feared, for they impose on all men the laws of a personality which can exist but once. They are a devouring force; they illumine, but they burn; they have the right to be unique in their being and in their work. They seem to realise in themselves the whole aim of nature, and there is nothing left for those who follow but to be absorbed and disappear.

It would be absurd to offer Michelangelo as a model to young artists. Should great men ever be taken as models in art? Is not that one of the errors of classical training? They are examples of energy, sources of force and beauty. It is well to look for a moment on their radiance, then tear ourselves from their contemplation and work.

"the Dutch Michelangelo," Frans Floris, "the Flemish Michelangelo," and their innumerable followers, not to mention the French and Spanish imitators, the Fréminets and the Cespedès.

Chronological Table

DATE	IMPORTANT EVENTS	PRINCIPAL WORKS
1475	March 6. Birth of Michelangelo at Caprese.	
1488	April 1. He enters the school of Domenico and David Ghirlandajo.	
1489	He enters the school of Bertoldo and becomes the protégé of Lorenzo de' Medici.	
1490–1492	. . . .	*Mask of a Faun.* *Madonna of the Stairs.* *Combat of the Centaurs.*
1492	April 8. Death of Lorenzo de' Medici.	
1492–1494	In the service of Piero de' Medici.	Wooden crucifix. Statue of *Hercules.*
1494	October. Flight to Venice and Bologna. He worked at S. Petronio in Bologna.	Angel for the Arca of S. Domenico in Bologna.
1495	Return to Florence.	*Giovannino.* *Sleeping Love.*
1496	June 25. Arrival in Rome.	*Bacchus.* *Cupid.*
1498	May 23. Savonarola is burned in Florence.	

1498–1500......................	Pietà of St. Peter's.
1501 Return to Florence.	Statues for the Piccolomini altar in the cathedral of Sienna.
1501–1505......................	*David.*
	Cartoon for the battle of Cascina.
	Holy Family of Agnolo Doni.
	Virgin of Bruges.
	Bas-reliefs of the Madonna for Taddeo Taddei and Bartolommeo Pitti.
1505 March. He is summoned to Rome by Julius II.	First plan for the tomb of Julius II.
1506 The Laocöon was discovered at Rome.	
1506 April 17. Flight to Florence.	
1506 End of November. Reconciliation with Julius at Bologna.	
1506–1508......................	Bronze statue of Julius II at Bologna.
1508 Return to Rome.	
1508 May 10 to 1512, October,....	Paintings on the ceiling of the Sistine.
1513 February 21. Death of Julius II.	
1513 March 11. Election of Leo X.	
1513 May 6. Second contract for the tomb of Julius II.	
1513–1516 Michelangelo at Florence.	*The Slaves.*
	Moses.
1516 July. Third contract for the tomb of Julius II.	
1517 September. Serious illness of Michelangelo.	
1518 January 19. Contract in regard to the façade of S. Lorenzo in Florence.	
1518–1520 Michelangelo at the quarries of Carrara, Seravezza.	

1520	March 10. Michelangelo is released from the contract for the façade of S. Lorenzo by an order from Leo X.	*The Christ* of the Minerva.
1520	April 6. Death of Raphael.	
1521	Beginning of the work on the chapel of the Medici at S. Lorenzo.	*The Madonna* of the chapel of the Medici.
1521	At the end of the year serious illness of Michelangelo.	*The Victory.*
1522	November 19. Election of Clement VII.	
1524–1526	Work on the tomb of the Medici and the Laurentian library.
1527	May 6. Capture of Rome by the Imperialists.	
1529	April 6. Michelangelo is named Governatore Generale and Procuratore of the fortifications of Florence. Mission to inspect the fortifications at Pisa, Livorno and Ferrara.	*Leda.*
1529	September 21. Flight to Venice. Siege of Florence.	
1529	November 20. Return to Florence. Defense of San Miniato.	
1530	August 12. Capitulation of Florence. Proscriptions.	*Apollo.*
1531	June. Serious illness of Michelangelo.	Work on the Medici tombs.
1532	April 29. Fourth contract for the monument of Julius II.	
1533	Beginning of the friendship with Tommaso dei Cavalieri in Rome.	First plan for the *Last Judgment.*
1534	Death in Florence of Lodovico, the father of Michelangelo.	
1534	September 23. Michelangelo returns to Rome, where he remains until his death.	

1534	September 25. Death of Clement VII.	
1534	October 13. Election of Paul III.	
1535	September 1. Michelangelo is named by order of Paul III architect-in-chief, sculptor and painter of the Apostolic Palace.	
1536	Beginning of the friendship with Vittoria Colonna at Rome.	
1536	April to November, 1541.....	*Last Judgment* in the Sistine.
1538	The statue of Marcus Aurelius is raised on the Capitoline.	*Brutus.* Drawings of Christ for Vittoria Colonna.
1542–1544......................		Frescoes of the Pauline Chapel.
1542	August 20. Last agreement for the monument of Julius II.	
1544	June. Serious illness of Michelangelo, who was cared for in the palace of the Strozzi.	
1545	February...................	Completion of the monument of Julius II in S. Pietro in Vinculi.
1545–1546 Titian in Rome.		
1546	January. Serious illness of Michelangelo. He gives the Slaves to the Strozzi.	Work on the cornice of the Farnese palace.
1547	January 1. Michelangelo named by Paul III architect of St. Peter's.	
1547	February 25. Death of Vittoria Colonna.	Work on the Capitol.
1549	November 10. Death of Paul III.	
1550	February 8. Election of Julius III.	Work on the Vigna del Papa Giulio and the reconstruction of the Belvedere stairway.

1551	First edition of the "Vite" of Vasari.	
1553	First edition of the life of Michelangelo by Ascanio Condivi.	Work on St. Peter's.
1555	March 23. Death of Julius III.	
1555	May 23. Election of Paul IV.	
1555	December 3. Death of Urbino, Michelangelo's servant.	The group of the *Pieta*, broken by Michelangelo, is continued and completed by Tiberio Calcagni.
1558	. . . .	He works at the model of the dome of St. Peter's.
1559–1560	Daniele da Volterra, at the command of Paul IV, paints drapery on the figures of the Last Judgment.	
1560	Catherine de' Medici requested Michelangelo to make the statue of Henri II.	Work on the transformation of the Baths of Diocletian into the church of S. Maria degli Angeli.
1561	August 29. Michelangelo was taken ill.	Work on the Porta Pia.
1563	January 31. Michelangelo made President of the Academy of Florence.	
1564	February.	*The Rondanini Pietà.*
1564	February 18. Death of Michelangelo.	
1564	July 14. Funeral at S. Lorenzo in Florence.	

Catalogue of the Principal Works of Michelangelo in Public Collections

I. Paintings
Italy
Florence. UFFIZI.
Holy Family, painted for Agnolo Doni (between 1501 and 1505).
Rome. VATICAN.
Paintings on the ceiling of the Sistine (1508–1512).
The Last Judgment (1536–1541).
The frescoes of the Pauline chapel (1542–1549).
England
London. NATIONAL GALLERY.
The Deposition (about 1495).
Madonna with Child and Infant St. John (about 1495).

II. Sculpture
Italy
Florence. MUSEO NAZIONALE.
Mask of a Faun (between 1490 and 1492).
Bacchus (1497).
The Dying Adonis (1497).
Virgin and Child, a circular bas-relief made for Taddeo Taddei (between 1501 and 1505).
Victory (1522–1523).
David Apollo (1526–1531).
Brutus (1538).

ACCADEMIA DELLE BELLE ARTI.

David (between 1501 and 1504).

CASA BUONARROTI.

Centaurs and Lapiths, bas-relief in marble (between 1490 and 1492).

Virgin and Child, bas-relief in bronze (between 1490 and 1492).

SAN LORENZO.

The Medici tombs (1524–1527 and 1530–1534).

SANTA MARIA DEI FIORE.

The Deposition (1553–1555).

Rome. SAINT PETER'S.

Pietà (1498–1500).

SAN PIETRO IN VINCOLI.

Tomb of Julius II: (*Moses,* 1513–1516).

Rachel and *Leah* (1542–1545).

France

Paris. THE LOUVRE.

The Slaves (1513–1516).

England

London. SOUTH KENSINGTON MUSEUM.

Kneeling Cupid (1497).

ROYAL ACADEMY.

Holy Family, circular bas-relief made for Bart. Pitti (between 1501 and 1505).

Belgium

Bruges. NOTRE DAME CATHEDRAL.

Madonna (between 1501 and 1505).

Note on the Drawings

The great European Museums—especially the Louvre, the Uffizi, the Albertina in Vienna, the British Museum, Oxford University and Windsor—contain very rich collections of Michelangelo's drawings. The most beautiful of those in the Louvre came from the Jabach and Mariette collections.

"You could not ask for anything more finished or showing a greater knowledge of drawing," says Mariette; . . . "they are almost too much finished. . . . I do not know any other master who finished his studies more completely. When he is looking for a certain pose he dashes off impetuously on the paper what comes from his imagination. He draws with large strokes. . . . But if he wants to study nature so that he may reproduce it later on in sculpture or in painting he follows an entirely different method. . . . His drawing is no longer a sketch, but a finished fragment in which no detail is left out, it is the flesh itself; and Michelangelo needed nothing more than this for his modelling. I have a number of drawings where you can see the marks which Michelangelo made on them, and which indicate that these designs were used by him as guides in his modelling. . . ."

Some of the drawings in the Louvre were for the tombs of the Medici and for the bronze David for Florimond Robertet.

Another curious thing about these drawings is that we often find upon them verses by Michelangelo, fragments of poems. Both verses and drawings are often the repetitions or variations of certain ideas which were in his mind for years and occupied his attention with the tenacity of fixed ideas.

Michelangelo used indifferently red chalk, pen and ink, and charcoal or pencil.

Bibliography

I. Writings of Michelangelo

Die Dichtungen des Michel-Angelo Buonarroti, herausgegeben und
 mit kritischem Apparat versehen von Carl FREY. Berlin, 1897
Le Rime, edited by Enzo Girardi BARI, 1961 (best chronology of
 the poems).
Le Lettere di Michel-Angelo Buonarroti, publicate, coi *Ricordi ed
 i Contratti artistici,* per cura di Gaetano MILANESI. Florence,
 1875, in-fol., IX, 721 pages. Lemonnier (495 letters, from 1497
 to 1563).
Rime di Michel-Angelo Buonarroti, raccolte da Michelagnolo suo
 nipote. Florence, 1623, Giunti (first complete edition, but full
 of errors).
Rime di Michel-Angelo Buonarroti, cavate dagli autografi e publicate da Cesare GUASTI. Florence, 1863 (first really accurate
 edition).

II. Works on Michelangelo

I. Writings of His Contemporaries.

Francesco BERNI, *Opere burlesche.* Florence, 1548. Giunti.
Benvenuto CELLINI, *Vita* (1559 to 1562), first edition. Naples,
 1728.—*I Trattati dell' oreficeria e della scultura.* Florence,
 1893, edition C. Milanesi.
Vittoria COLONNA, *Rime* (first edition). Parma, 1538;—(second
 edition), 1539;—(third edition), 1544;—edition SALTINI. Florence, 1860, Barbera.—*Carteggio,* published by Ermanno FER-
 RERO and Giuseppe MULLER. Turin, 1892, Loescher (Letters

153

and documents).—*Lettere inedite,* published by SALZA. Florence, 1898.—*Codice delle Rime di Vittoria Colonna,* appartenente a Margherita, regina di Navarra scoperto ed illustrato. Pistoia, 1900, ed. Tordi.

Ascanio CONDIVI, *Vita di Michel-Angelo Buonarroti.* Rome, 1553, Antonio BLADO;—(second edition). Florence, 1746, with notes by Mariette.

Donato GIANNOTTI, *De' giorni che Dante consumò nel cercare l'Inferno e' l Purgatorio. Dialoghi.* Florence, 1859.

Paolo GIOVIO, *Michaelis Angeli Vita,* published by TIRABOSCHI in his *Storia della letteratura italiana,* Vol. IX, Modena, 1781.

Donato GIANNOTTI, *De' giorni che Dante consumò nel cercare*

Francisco DE HOLLANDA, *Os Dialogos em Roma.* Porto, 1930.

François DE HOLLANDE, *Quatre Entretiens sur la Peinture,* held in Rome 1538 to 1539, written in 1548, published by Joachim DE VASCONCELLOS;—French translation in *Les Arts en Portugal,* by Count RACZYNSKI. Paris, 1846, Renouard.

Michelangelo's correspondents: I. *Sebastiano del Piombo,* Ed. Milanesi, French translation by A. LE PRIEUR. Paris, 1890, Librairie de l'Art.

Sammlung ausgewaehlter Biographien Vasaris, herausg. von Carl FREY (in the second volume are gathered *le Vite de Michel-Angelo Buonnaroti,* critical edition of all the biographies written by his contemporaries).

Benedetto VARCHI, *Due lezioni di Benedetto Varchi.* Florence, 1549.—*Orazione funerale recitata nelle esequie di Michel-Angelo Buonarroti.* Florence, 1564, Giunti.

Giorgio VASARI, *Vite degli architetti, pittori e scultori* (first edition). Florence, 1550, in 4to;—(second edition). Florence, 1568, in 4to.—edition of MILANESI. Florence, 1856, Lemonnier.

Blaise DE VIGENERE, *Les Images de Philostrate.* Paris, 1629.

II. Modern Works

Charles BLANC, George DUPLESSIS, Charles GARNIER, Louis GONSE, Eug. GUILLAUME, Paul MANTZ, A. MEZIERES and Anatole DE MONTAIGLON. *L'Oeuvre et la Vie de Michel-Ange.* Paris, Gazette des Beaux-Arts, 1876.

Robert J. CLEMENTS, *Michelangelo's Theory of Art.* New York, 1961.

Richard DUPPA, *The Life and Literary Works of Michel-Angelo Buonarroti.* London, 1806, 1816 (translations in verse of the poetry of Michelangelo by Southey and Wordsworth).

Carl FREY, *Studien zu Michelagnolo (Jahrb. der K. preuss. Kunstssamml.)* Berlin, 1895–1896.

Giovanni GAYE, *Carteggio inedito d'artisti dei secoli XIV, XV, XVI.* Florence, 1839, Three volumes.

Baron H. GEYMULLER, *Michelangelo als Architekt.*

Aurelio GOTTI, *Vita di Michel-Angelo.* Florence, 1875, two volumes.

Albert HAUCK, *Vittoria Colonna.* Heidelberg, 1882.

Valerio MARIANI, *La Poesia di Michelangelo.* Rome, 1941.

Charles MORGAN, *Michelangelo.* New York, 1960.

Giovanni PAPINI, *La Vita di Michelangelo nella Vita del suo tempo.* Milan, 1949.

Luigi PASSERINI, *La bibliografia di Michel-Angelo Buonarroti e gli incisori delle sue opere.* Florence, 1875.

Quatremere DE QUINCY, *Histoire de la vie et des ouvrages de Michel-Ange Buonarroti.* Paris, 1835.

F. REISET, *Notice des dessins du musée du Louvre.* Paris, 1866.

Alfred VON REUMONT, *Vittoria Colonna.* Fribourg, 1881.

Corrado RICCI, *Michelangelo.* Florence, 1901.

Fr. Al RIO, *Michel-Ange et Raphael* (first edition). Hanover, 1860 (since then there have been seven editions; the last appeared in 1900 with illustrations).

Romain ROLLAND, *Michel-Ange.* Paris, 1905.

Romain ROLLAND, *Vie de Michel-Ange.* Paris, 1906.

Anton SPRINGER, *Raffael und Michelangelo,* 1878. 1e volume Munich, 1901, 2e volume Munich, 1905.

Dr. Ernst STEINMANN, *Die Sixtinische Kapelle.*

John Addington SYMONDS, *The Life of Michel-Angelo Buonarroti.* London, 1893.

Charles DE TOLNAY, *Michelangelo.* Princeton, 1947, Six volumes.

Henry THODE, *Michel-Angelo und das Ende der Renaissance.* 1e volume Berlin, 1902, 2e volume Berlin, 1903.

C. Heath WILSON, *Life and Works of Michel-Angelo.* London, 1876.

Index

157